ECOLOGY, LAW
and
ECONOMICS

The Simple Analytics of Natural Resource
and Environmental Economics

Nicholas Mercuro
Franklin A. López
Kristian P. Preston

UNIVERSITY
PRESS OF
AMERICA

Lanham • New York • London

Library of Congress Cataloging-in-Publication Data
Mercuro, Nicholas.
Ecology, law and economics : the simple analytics of natural
resource and environmental economics / Nicholas Mercuro, Franklin
A. López and Kristian P. Preston.
p.   cm.
1. Environmental policy.   2. Natural resources—Management.
3. Environmental economics.   4. Environmental law.   I. López,
Franklin A.   II. Preston, Kristian P.   III. Title.
GE170.M46   1994   363.7—dc20   94–17739 CIP

ISBN 0–8191–9593–6 (cloth : alk. paper)
ISBN 0–8191–9594–4 (pbk. : alk. paper)

GE170
.M46
1994

ACKNOWLEDGEMENTS

UNO's Urban Waste Management and Research Center

Partial financial support for *ECOLOGY, LAW AND ECONOMICS* was provided by the Urban Waste Management and Research Center (U.W.M.R.C.) at the University of New Orleans. The U.W.M.R.C. was established as an academic center of excellence to address urban environmental issues. Through a cooperative agreement with the U.S. Environmental Protection Agency, the center conducts activities in the development of research, education, and outreach programs that emphasize an integrated multimedia approach to waste management and pollution prevention.

I am greatly indebted to Professor Herman E. Koenig and Professor William E. Cooper both of Michigan State University for many of the core ideas contained in this book as originally set forth in the *Ecosystems Design and Management Program*. In this regard I must acknowledge the Jessie Smith Noyes Foundation for their generous financial support throughout my graduate studies. In addition, I gratefully acknowledge the German Fulbright Commission for their generous support with a special thanks to my environmental economics students -- from both the American Studies Institute of the Free University of Berlin (Spring 1993) and from the University of New Orleans (Fall 1993) for their very helpful comments on earlier drafts of chapters of this book.*N.M.*

My contributions to this book were written while I was at the *Instituto de Desarrollo Empresarial* of Guayaquil, Ecuador on sabbatical leave from the *University of New Orleans*. I am most grateful to both institutions for their financial and intellectual support. A special thanks are due to Pablo A. López and Aricia Rener who made valuable editing suggestions to my contributions to this book. *F.A.L.*

I wish to thank the late W.E. Westman for his insights into the application of ecological principles to environmental policy-level issues and decision making. I also wish to thank the students in my environmental impact assessment and plant ecology classes for their valuable feedback regarding some of concepts covered in my contributions to this book.*K.P.P.*

Finally, we thank Sunny Francois and Greg Jackson for their technical support in preparing this manuscript for publication; and special thanks to J. Taliancich for help with Figures II.3 and II.8.

CONTENTS

CHAPTER I: INTRODUCTION & THE ECONOMY

CHAPTER II: THE NATURAL SYSTEM

CHAPTER III: THE STATE

CHAPTER IV: THE ECONOMICS OF NATURAL RESOURCES

CHAPTER V: ENVIRONMENTAL ECONOMIC REMEDIES

CHAPTER I

INTRODUCTION
&
THE ECONOMY

INTRODUCTION

The purpose of this book is to present a conceptual model that describes the interrelations among the (1) the economy, (2) the ecology of the natural system, and (3) the state (including law and the government broadly understood). From this vantage point, the policy role of environmental economics and natural resource economics can be better understood thereby providing a deeper appreciation of both the challenges before us and the variety of remedies for solving environmental and natural resource problems that are now available.

From the outset two points must be made clear. The first concerns the role of and reliance on technology and population control to solve the natural resource and environmental problems of the many nations of the world. The position taken in this book is that the nations of the world can not solely rely on the so-called "technological fix" or some magical solution the population problem. We, like most who share our concern about the future of our environment, advocate the continuation of technological breakthroughs as well as policies that attempt to control the growth of pollution, the exhaustion of natural resources, and the dangers of an exploding population. However, for the immediate future, this book takes the position that there are a host of policies as to the environment and natural resources that can be formulated and implemented without delay. Our modest aim is simply to demonstrate to those who are concerned with our natural resources and the environment, the way in which economics (both in substance as well as a way of thinking about these problems) might help to resolve these problems in a manner consistent with the efficient allocation of society's scarce resources.

The second point to note is that we take the position that the persons living within the society are not just other living organisms in the ecosystem. They have the distinguishing combined characteristics of (1) intelligence, (2) volition and (3) the capacity to act. In the simplest of terms, for the purposes of this book, what man did at Chernobl is quite different from fish devouring each other within a food chain.

The remainder of this chapter will present a description of the economy with an emphasis on understanding the nature of the flows inherent in the economic system. The economy is presented as a man-made system of social control -- a socially structured process dedicated to the material transformation of society's natural resources into commodities -- goods and services -- designed to satisfy the needs and wants of the individuals that make up that society.

Chapter II is intended to provide the reader with a synoptic review of the structure and function of ecosystems with an emphasis on the flows inherent in the biogeochemical cycles. In addition, the interrelations between the economy and the natural system are explored.

Chapter III presents an abstract view of the state that concentrates on the role of government at the constitutional stage of choice, on the political/legal decision-making processes -- the institutional stage of choice, and, the consequent economic impacts of the legal relations governing society -- the economic impact stage of choice. In addition, the interrelations among the economy, the natural system, and the state are explored.

Chapters IV and V, respectively present the simple economic analytics of natural resource economics and environmental economics. The material in these two chapters undertakes a review of several of the natural resource and environmental economic remedies available to a society to help regulate the extraction of natural resources and to abate pollution. The focus is on the theoretical approaches developed within the fields of natural resource and environmental economics. We are fully aware that many other disciplines including political science, philosophy, law, administrative planning, the natural sciences, sociology,...etc. have their own unique contributions to make with respect to understanding natural resource and environmental issues and in proposing alternative solutions.[1]

Within the marketplace of ideas, we encourage colleagues from all disciplines, from their unique and valuable perspectives, to contribute to the base of knowledge and to move forward by advancing their own remedies based on whatever guiding principles and values (such as justice or fairness...etc.) they think may help in this important and continuing debate on how to sustain the ecological integrity of our unique environment. In Chapters IV and V, we are trying only to describe how policies might be fashioned if one were interested in incorporating economic efficiency considerations into the formulation of remedies to moderate the rate of extraction of resources or to help abate pollution. The most basic economic principle of comparative advantage suggests that we leave the discussion of remedies based on the ideas of justice and fairness (those proffered by other disciplines) to others more qualified.

THE ECONOMY

CIRCULAR FLOW OF ECONOMIC ACTIVITY

The intellectual construct to depict the *economy* in this simplified model is that of perfect competition. The interrelations and flows inherit in a perfectly competitive economy are best seen in the standard circular flow diagram (see Figure I.1).[2] Here, the privately owned scarce resources (land, labor and capital) are allocated through factor markets to firms which, in turn, produce goods and services to satisfy the demands of consumers. With respect to the workings of the economy, for economists, the major concern is with its allocative efficiency -- the extent to which the aggregate collection of commodities (both goods and services) produced in the economy best satisfies the wants and desires of the individuals in the society. Given the significance of the role of the economy, it is useful to explore the conditions both for (a) its success, and (b) the reasons for market failure. As to the latter, it is the concept of *externalities* that is at center stage.

THE ECONOMY, THE MARKET AND EXTERNALITIES

In introducing the concept of externalities we start with a definition from Bernard Huber which reflects the current and broadly accepted usage of the concept of externality in conventional neoclassical economics.

> An *economic externality* may be viewed as an economic gain or loss accruing to one or more recipient agents as a result of an economic action initiated by another agent -- with the gain or loss not being reflected in the market price. The initiating or the recipient economic agent may be either a producer or consumer (Huber, 1979:36).

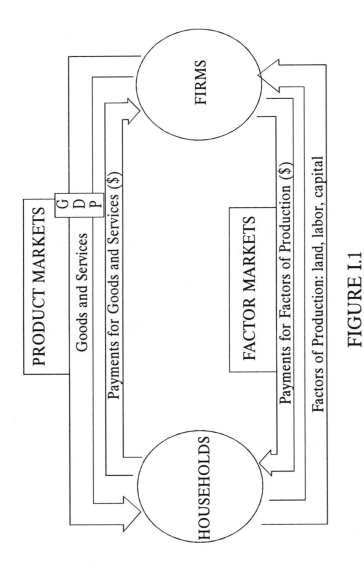

FIGURE I.1

Thus, an externality exists when the action of one consumer or producer enters the utility function or the production function of some other consumer or producer, respectively.

Defining an externality in this conventional sense focuses attention on economic activity in the private market sector and the functioning or disfunctioning of the *purely competitive market*. The purely competitive perfectly functioning market has the following characteristics: (a) many buyers motivated by self-interest acting to maximize utility; (b) many sellers also motivated by self-interest acting to maximize profits in atomistic industries or contestable markets; (c) individual buyers and sellers are unable to exert any control over market prices and are thus, price takers; (d) prices serve as the guideposts for decision makers in the market to communicate scarcity; (e) products are standardized (i.e., homogeneous); (f) there are no barriers to entry or exit, thus, consumers and producers are free to enter or leave all product and factor markets; (g) all buyers and sellers are fully informed as to the terms of all market transactions; (h) resources are held in private property with all rights defined and assigned; and (i) prevailing laws and property rights are fully enforced through the state.

THE CONCEPT OF MARKET FAILURE[3]

Given the vast literature that relates to market failure and the concept of externality as it relates to natural resource and environmental economics, a more formal analysis of the market sector is in order. From society's standpoint, the significance of having marginal social benefit (MBs) equal to marginal social cost (MCs) is best grasped by understanding what transpires when this equality does *not* hold. Consider Figure I.2 where the MBs and MCs for some good X are depicted. If the allocation of resources is such that quantity X_1 gets produced, then the MBs exceeds MCs for that quantity of good X. As additional resources are devoted to the production of good X, society would incrementally gain benefits in excess of costs as more and more X is produced and consumed.

Once the quantity Xo is produced no further incremental gains are possible, i.e., once MBs = MCs, society is said to have achieved a Pareto efficient allocation of those resources devoted to good X. Had society allowed X_1 to continue to be produced (where MBs > MCs), it would then be said, with respect to good X, there would be a "persistent underalloction of resources." However, if society had continued to devote additional resources to good X and had instead produced X_2, then the MCs would have exceeded the MBs. Clearly, each additional unit of X produced and consumed beyond Xo would entail incremental costs in excess of the incremental benefits; in this case (whenever MCs > MBs) it would be said that there is a "persistent overallocation of resources." By foregoing these additional units of good X and remaining at Xo (that quantity of good X which equates MBs to MCs) as stated above, society is said to achieve a Pareto efficient allocation of resources. By allowing perfectly competitive markets for all goods (X, Y, Z...Nth good) to clear, society achieves a Pareto optimal allocation of resources throughout the entire economy. Again, the important point to be underscored is that when all benefits and costs are accounted for, that is, when MBs = MCs for all goods in the economy, the outcome is said to be Pareto efficient.

There is an additional important concept related to the concept of efficiency and that is the duality theorem (Feldman, 1980:47-58; O'Connell:9-33). The theorem states that barring major problems with public goods and externalities, a purely competitive, perfectly functioning market will achieve a Pareto efficient allocation of resources. This correspondence between the purely competitive market performance and Pareto efficiency is predicated on the economy meeting four necessary conditions. These conditions are summarized in Table I.1.[4] As indicated above, the condition for a Pareto efficient allocation of resources of society's scarce resources is that the MBs = MCs for each and every good.

Initially we will assume that the market sector is society's sole means of social control for the allocation of society's scarce resources (this is relaxed latter in Chapter III - The State). With the market as *the* means for allocating resources, all decisions are made by individual consumers and producers attempting to maximize utility and profits, respectively. In order to achieve an efficient outcome through the market, it is necessary that the four conditions set forth in the Table I.1 be fulfilled. In doing so, the market solutions generated, will take into account all social benefits and social costs. A brief, but closer look at each of these four conditions is necessary to fully understand the meaning of market failure and its ultimate significance for economic-based remedies for environmental problems.

The reason for this close scrutiny, is that the market sector will fail to generate a Pareto optimal outcome if any one of the four conditions is not met. That is, deviations or departures from the basic structural characteristics of the purely competitive market will drive a wedge into any one or more of the four basic equalities. As a consequence, the overall condition for Pareto efficiency (MBs = MCs, the summary equation) will not be met. In reality, there are a variety of factors and forces at work in the economy that create such inequalities and several (especially those related to condition 4) have a direct bearing on the thrust of natural resource and environmental economics. It is to an examination of these four conditions we now turn.

Conditions

$$(1) \qquad MB_S = MB_P$$

$$(2) \qquad MB_P = P$$

$$(3) \qquad P = MC_P$$

$$(4) \qquad MC_P = MC_S$$

$$\boxed{MB_S \quad = \quad MC_S}$$

Pareto Efficient Condition

where, MB_S = marginal social benefit

MB_P = marginal private benefits

P = market price

MC_P = marginal private costs

MC_S = marginal social costs

TABLE I.1

(1) Condition #1

With respect to condition (1) shown in Table I.1, Pareto efficiency requires that marginal social benefits (all benefits) be accounted for, while utility maximization in a market economy assumes the consumers consider only private benefits. Thus, achieving condition (1) MBs = MBp would be consistent in those instances where all social benefits will be accounted for in the market sector by the activities of individual consumers. The meaning of the fulfillment of condition (1) MBs = MBp, can be intuitively grasped by considering what occurs when an individual consumes a steak for dinner. The incremental benefit society acquires by this private market action is probably not much different than the incremental benefit the individual acquires in eating the steak -- the individual benefits by so much and society benefits by that same incremental amount.

However, there are many situations in which society's incremental benefits differ from the benefits acquired by an individual when that individual undertakes a particular market transaction. Instances where the benefits accruing to society exceed the benefits gained by an individual include an individual engaging in such activities as (a) having his home landscaped and gardened, (b) having the family inoculated for contagious diseases, or (c) seeing that children acquire an education (assuming here that all education is only privately provided). In each case the individual acquires a marginal private benefit (MBp) plus, there is an external benefit (XB) conferred on some others (others who are not part of the transaction). These examples can be depicted in Figure I.3 where MBs equals the summation of the private consumption benefits (MBp) plus the external benefits (XB) accruing to other members of society as a result of the private consumption decision, MBs = MBp + XB.

As is evident in the figure, from society's standpoint, the optimal or efficient allocation of society's resources would be at Xo units of good X where MBs = MCs. However, consumers and producers in the market make private, not social decisions, and thus will make decisions with regard to *private* benefit assessments (along MBp) resulting in a solution where MBp = MCs. This outcome corresponds to a nonoptimal, persistent underallocation of resources at point X_1, where it is observed that MBs > MBp, a violation of condition (1).

(2) Condition #2

Condition (2), MBp = P, states that the price an individual consumer is willing to pay to acquire a good reflects perfectly his private marginal benefit derived from the good. In fulfilling this condition, each individual is maximizing his utility. Furthermore, these prices are the ones that will guide producers to allocate more or less resources to the production of various goods and thereby

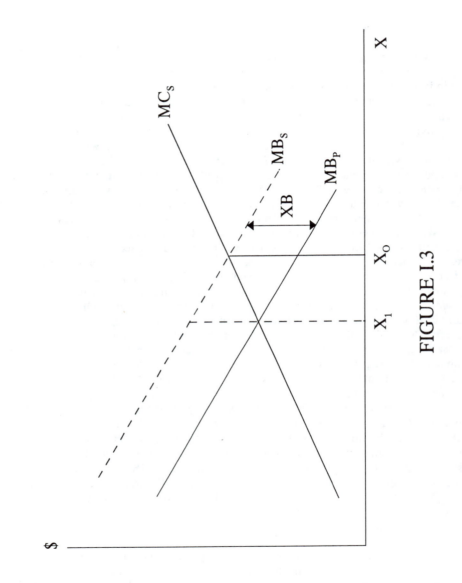

FIGURE I.3

take into account the marginal private benefit assessments of the consumers.

With respect to condition (2), MBp = P, it is difficult to imagine violations of this condition for consumers in the market for final goods and services. However, monopsonists in resource markets (i.e., a single buyer or association of buyers with some control over the factor price) do violate this condition.

An example of a monopsonistic firm in the labor market is depicted in Figure I.4. This example requires some redefinitions as we shift to the labor market. In the labor market, price (P) is now the price of labor (P_L) or simply the wage rate, W. MBp, the private gain to the firm is represented as the marginal revenue product to the firm for employing additional laborers, MRP_L, and is assumed equal to MBs. MCs becomes MRCs, society's marginal resource cost, and represents the true opportunity cost incurred by society in supplying additional units of labor (MCs is the supply of labor curve). And finally, MCp = MRCp represents the private marginal expense to the firm in acquiring additional units of labor, the firm's private marginal resource cost. From society's standpoint, the efficient solution would dictate that the firm hire Lo laborers (where MBs = MCs) and pay Wo wage rate -- where Wo = MRP_L (rewritten in terms of Condition 2 -- Table I.1, P = MBp). However, the firm in making its decision on how many laborers to hire will consider only the private cost of hiring additional laborers (i.e., move along MRCp) and hire L_1 laborers (where MRC_L = MRP_L) and pay W_1 wage rate. Thus, the market solution under monopsony will come to rest at L_1 units of labor (with a persistent underallocation of resources) where it is observed W_1 < MRP_L (that is, rewritten in terms of Condition 2 -- Table I.1, P < MBp), a violation of condition (2).

(3) Condition #3

Condition (3), P = MCp, states that the price received by a producer perfectly reflects the marginal private cost of producing the good, i.e., the market price equals the opportunity cost of using the resources needed to produce the good. In fulfilling this condition, each firm is maximizing its profits under perfect competition.

With respect to condition (3), P = MCp, recall that in a perfectly competitive market each firm acts as a price taker which means that each firm perceives that it has no control over product price. Each firm, within a limited range, can sell as much or as little of the good as it wants at the prevailing market price. As a result, the marginal revenue (MR) of one additional unit sold is equal to the market price, (i.e., MR = P). Since profit maximizing firms will always produce at a level of output where their private marginal cost of the next unit is equal to the marginal revenue of that unit (MCp = MR), and since in a

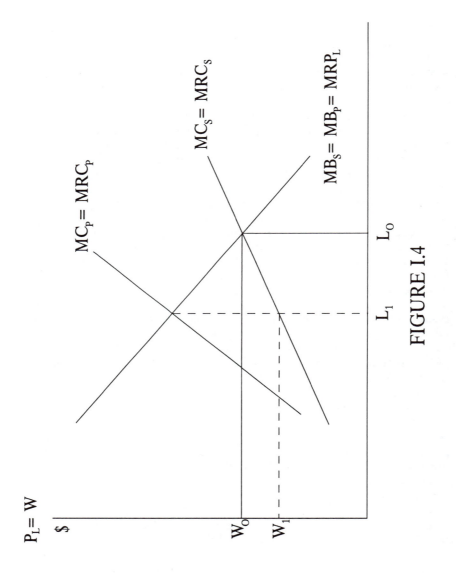

FIGURE I.4

perfectly competitive industry (MR = P), firms will produce at an output level where price is equal to marginal private cost thus, condition (3), P = MCp, is met.

Violations of condition (3) occur in cases of imperfect competition where firms, to some extent, exert control over the market price (Figure I.5). Typically, this is what transpires in various degrees in the market structures of pure monopoly, oligopoly and monopolistic competition. Firms in these market structures typically face a downward sloping demand curve, which implies that the marginal revenue of the next unit sold (the firm's MBp curve) is less than the price for each quantity produced and sold (MR < P). As depicted (in Figure I.5), efficiency would dictate that Xo units be produced and sold at price Po, where MBs = MCs. However, the firm, acting privately to maximize it profits, will move along its marginal revenue curve and produce that output that equates marginal revenue, MR to its marginal private cost, MCp, and produce X_1 units and charge price P_1. As a result, the profit maximizing firm with market power sufficient to affect price will systematically underallocate resources and produce at a level of output where price exceeds marginal private cost; that is, since P > MR and the firm produces that level of output where MR = MCp, then P > MCp, a violation of condition (3).

(4) Condition #4

Finally, since Pareto efficiency requires that all marginal social costs be considered and profit maximization assumes that the producers consider only private costs, then condition (4) MCp = MCs describes those market transactions where all social costs will be accounted for in the market sector by the activities of individual producers.

The fulfillment of condition (4), MCp = MCs, can be illustrated by the example of the organic farm that avoids the use of any nonorganic fertilizers, pesticides or rodenticides. The implication is that all of the marginal private costs incurred to produce the farm products are equivalent to all of the marginal social costs incurred by society - that is, there are no external costs. Violations of condition (4) are a result of (a) the interdependencies often brought on by the existence of common property resources, (b) technological interdependencies, (c) interdependencies due to the location or proximity of individuals, and (d) unenforced government rights and regulations. For purposes of Chapter IV and V, the class of externalities associated with the violation of condition (4) is the most important and widely discussed case, for it includes such phenomena as air and water pollution, noise pollution and the exhaustion of natural resources.

Exploring this in some detail, firms make their output decisions on the basis of the costs of production that result from the purchase of privately owned

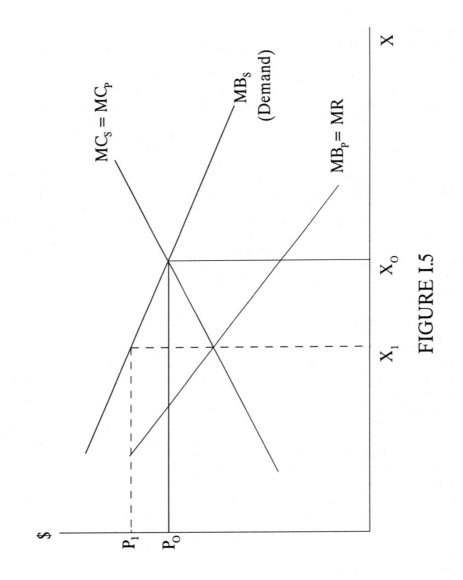

FIGURE I.5

factors of production, as expressed by the firm's marginal private costs (MCp). However, in cases where the firm utilizes a common property resource (and supply does not exceed demand at a zero price), the production of a good entails costs that are not borne by the firm but are borne by other producers or consumers in the society, yielding an external cost, XC (see Figure I.6). The marginal social cost, MCs, equals the sum of the marginal private cost plus the external cost (MCs = MCp + XC). From society's standpoint, the efficient allocation of resources would coincide with the production and consumption of Xo units of good X where MBs = MCs. However, the perfectly competitive firm will maximize profits by considering only private costs, moving along MCp, resulting in a solution where MBs = MCp. This corresponds to a nonoptimal, overallocation of resources at point X_1, where it is observed that MCs > MCp, a violation of condition (4).

(5) Other Sources of Market Failure to Note

There are two other notable sources of market failure, one concerning information, the other concerning the enforcement of rights. Both the lack of full information to market participants and the lack of complete enforcement of rights can drive a wedge into anyone of the equalities given by the four conditions specified in Table I.1.

Recall that one of the basic assumptions of a purely competitive, perfectly functioning market is that all consumers and producers have perfect information over all facets of all market transactions. However, if the requirement of perfect information is not met, then conditions arise that can serve to drive a wedge into the equalities given presented in Table I.1 and especially in conditions (2) and (3) and, thereby prevent the market from attaining a Pareto optimal outcome. For example, if a consumer is not fully informed as to the actual benefits to be derived from the acquisition of additional units of the good, then the price he is willing to pay for the good in an attempt to maximize his utility will likely be at variance with the benefits received. That is, the benefits received will not equal the price the consumer is willing to pay, MBp ≠ P, since the price was based on an incorrect or incomplete assessment due to a lack of full information.

The specific impact upon the individual consumer brought on by the lack of full information can be to the consumer's benefit or detriment. If the impact on the consumer was to his benefit then MBp may exceed P, for example, the unanticipated discovery of oil on the site of a newly acquired vacation home. Whereas, if the impact was to his detriment then MBp be less than P. An example might be the unknown side-effects of medications. In either case MBp ≠ P, which would preclude a Pareto-efficient outcome.

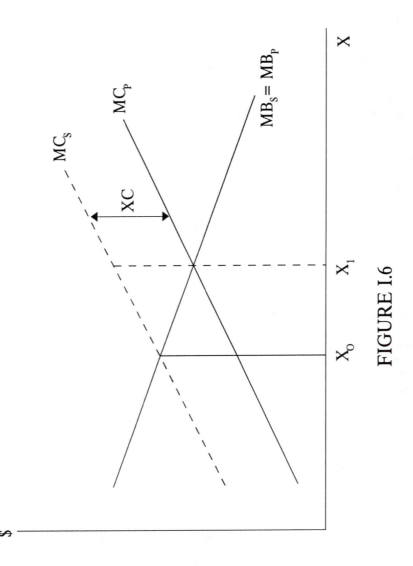

FIGURE I.6

In a similar manner, a producer who lacks perfect information, say with respect to market demand, scarcity of resources, or technology, in an attempt to maximize profits, is likely to make output decisions that are at variance with the actual costs incurred, resulting in P $\neq$ MCp. If the actual market demand for a producer's product, and therefore the market price, is not fully known due to a lack of perfect information, then the true market price may be greater or less than the producer's assessment of that price. In either case, P $\neq$ MCp, which prevents the attainment of a Pareto efficient solution.

The complete governmental enforcement of rights is another of the basic assumptions of purely competitive markets. The full enforcement of rights pertaining to contracts is one of the prerequisites for the smooth functioning of purely competitive markets. Once private property rights are defined and assigned, then the subsequent lack of protection of these rights underlying the market sector can drive a wedge into any one of the four conditions and thereby prevent the market from attaining a Pareto optimal outcome. A simple example of the impact on allocative efficiency as a result on nonenforcement of rights as related to each of the four conditions will make this apparent.

The lack of enforcement of rights leading to a violation of condition (1) MBs = MBp, can be illustrated by the case of an individual who, for his own fishing enjoyment, stocks his private lake with fish. If anti-poaching or trespass laws are not enforced, then MBs > MBp. Condition (2), MBp = P, will be violated if laws that allow for the establishment of unions to countervail monopsony power are not enforced; as a result, MRP_L > W (i.e., MBp > P). Condition (3), P = MCp, will be violated if antitrust laws go unenforced, i.e., P > MCp. And finally, condition (4), MCp = MCs, will be violated if environmental or nuisance laws that prohibit firms from discharging smoke into the air are not enforced, MCp < MCs.

SEVERAL PRELIMINARY POINTS TO NOTE REGARDING THE ECONOMY

• As established above, from the duality theorem, if markets are reasonably competitive ("barring major problems with public goods and externalities"), we know that the market will yield a Pareto efficient allocation of society's resources.

• An increase in GDP -- the total value of all final goods and services produced in an economy during a given year -- which is to say, annual economic growth, entails an increase in the flow rates within the circular flow diagram.

● There is the obvious, but often overlooked fact that each nation's *economy* -- for a variety of reasons including (a) historical, (b) technological, (c) political, and above all, (d) its geography, including its environment, climate, natural resources base...etc., has a unique, nation-specific *spatial arrangement*. That is, given the above four factors, each economy produces a unique spatial pattern of development -- urban areas, agricultural use, areas industrial zones, wilderness areas...etc. dictating a unique air, land, and water use pattern within the borders of that nation.

● Finally, the *economy* can be viewed as a man-made system of social control -- a socially structured process dedicated to the material transformation of society's scarce air, land, and water resources into commodities -- goods and services -- designed to satisfy the needs and wants of the individuals that make up that society. In this sense, the real material transformation flows are driven by the dollar flows within the established markets with those dollar flows as expressions of the values reflected in the market economy.

ENDNOTES

1. On the role of economics in helping to resolve issues regarding both the environment and natural resources see Johnson,(1988:1-18).

2. The standard circular flow diagram presented here is the same as that presented in the introductory chapter of virtually any introductory principles of economics textbook.

3. This discussion of market failure draws on an earlier formulation by Mercuro and Ryan,(1984).

4. A similar table was initially presented in Wonnacott and Wonnacott,(1979:178-194).

REFERENCES

Feldman, A.M. 1980. *Welfare Economics and Social Choice Theory*. Boston: Martinus Nijhoff Publishing.

Huber, B.P. 1979. *Modern Public Finance*. Homewood,IL: Richard D. Irwin, Inc.

Johnson, G.M. 1988. The Role of Economics in Natural Resource and Environmental Policy Analysis. In *Natural Resource and Environmental Policy Analysis: Cases in Applied Economics*, eds. G.M. Johnston, D. Freshwater, and P. Favero. Boulder: Westview Press: 1-18.

Mercuro, N. and Ryan, T. 1984. *Law, Economics and Public Policy*. Greenwich, CT: JAI Press.

O'Connell, J.F. 1982. *Welfare Economic Theory*. Boston: Auburn House Publishing Co.

Wonnacott, P. and Wonnacott, R. 1979. *Introduction to Microeconomics*. Homewood,IL: Richard D. Irwin, Inc.

CHAPTER II

THE NATURAL SYSTEM

INTRODUCTION

Ecology, the study of natural systems, is interestingly derived from the same Greek root as economics. While the latter deals primarily with the management of human behavior, ecology is the science or study of living organisms and their environment (both energy and matter). The realm of ecology is best visualized by examining the levels of biological organization of matter (Figure II.1). The organismic, population, community, ecosystem, and ecosphere levels all fall within the scope of ecology. Here the term population refers to a group of organisms of the same species while a community consists of a group of populations within a given area (e.g., a stream community consisting of different populations of fish, aquatic plants, insects, amphibians, and microorganisms). The ecosystem, the level of most interest, is then a collection of communities and the interactions within them and the physical environment. The ecosphere which consists of all living organisms on the planet and the physical environment in which they live has three major components each of which will be discussed in turn. The lithosphere is the solid surface of the planet consisting largely of rock and soil. By contrast, the hydrosphere is the liquid portion of the earth's surface and consists of water bodies including the oceans, lakes, and rivers. The atmosphere is the gaseous layer surrounding the planet and extends approximately 120 km (75 miles) from the earth's surface. While the atmosphere is made up of four distinct layers, the lower two are of greatest consequence for living organisms. About 75% of the mass of the planet's air is found in the troposphere which extends approximately 17 km (11 miles) from the surface. The most abundant gases in the troposphere are nitrogen (78%), oxygen (21%), and carbon dioxide (0.036%). The stratosphere extends from 17 km to

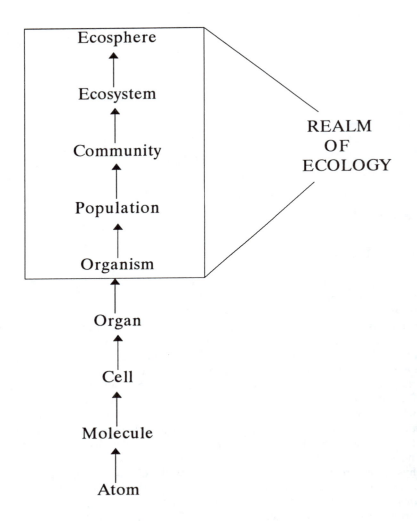

FIGURE II.1 Biological Organization Of Matter

50 km (approximately 11 - 31 miles) above the earth's surface. The ozone layer (discussed below in the climate section) which screens harmful ultra-violet radiation is found in the lower stratosphere between 17 km to 26 km (11 - 16 miles) from the earth's surface. These two atmospheric layers differ in another fundamental way; while temperature decreases with altitude in the troposphere just the opposite occurs in the stratosphere. Temperature once again decreases with altitude in the mesosphere (50 - 80 km) and then finally increases with altitude in the thermosphere (80 - 120 km), the outermost layer of the atmosphere.

Unlike most other disciplines that typically are reductionist in nature, ecology is "holistic" in that it examines not only the biotic and abiotic components of a system but also the interactions among those components. This type of an approach is especially useful when examining the effects of anthropogenic (i.e., human induced) stressors and disturbance. In many cases a seemingly small (or even initially benign) effect in the short-term may, due to the complexity of the interactions within a system, manifest itself into a significant deleterious (and often costly) outcome in the long-term.

The products or tangible features of natural ecosystems (and in many cases modified systems such as agriculture) which are typically available for human activity are known as ecosystem structures. They include living organisms such as plants and animals as well as nonliving features such as soil nutrient stocks, minerals, and fossil fuels. Humans may derive economic benefits by harvesting or mining structures such as timber, fish, oil, and minerals. Alternatively, humans also derive benefits from the use of intact structures through recreation and aesthetic activities. Structures are the standing stock of an ecosystem and collectively are nature's free "goods" (Westman, 1977). Obviously the type, quantity, and availability of these goods for economic activity varies from region to region and are determined by the area's productivity and limiting factors. In contrast to structures, ecosystem functions are dynamic processes such as energy fixation, nutrient cycling, soil binding, gas absorption and release, or decomposition. These processes cannot be harvested or enjoyed in the same fashion as ecosystem structures. However, they nonetheless maintain clean air and water, a green planet, and a balance among living organisms and can be considered nature's free "services" (Westman, 1977). While these goods and services are free, there are definite costs to society when ecosystems are disturbed by human activities and ecosystem structures and functions are disrupted or destroyed entirely.

MATTER AND ENERGY EXCHANGE

Ecosystem processes and interactions are manifested by a series of matter and energy exchanges. Living organisms and ecosystems are ordered systems and maintain their order through a complex set of homeostatic mechanisms. These mostly negative feedback mechanisms maintain the homeostasis or dynamic balance of systems through sets of opposing and compensating adjustments which respond to the physical laws of matter and energy. Moreover, these laws form the foundation for understanding the exchanges of matter and energy at every level of biological organization.

(1) Law of Conservation of Matter

Although the earth loses gas molecules to space and gains matter from space in the form of cosmic dust and meteorites these losses and gains are negligible compared to the earth's total mass. The earth thus has the same amount of matter it will ever have. This balance of matter is a consequence of the law of conservation of matter which simply states that matter can be neither created or destroyed but can be changed from one form into another. Physical and chemical changes can thus rearrange the spatial pattern and combination of atoms but cannot create or destroy them. The ultimate implication of this law is that there is no true "disposal" or "throwing away" of wastes generated by economic or other anthropogenic activities. Everything "thrown away" or "disposed of" by society remains in the environment in some form or another.

(2) Laws of Thermodynamics

a. First Law of Thermodynamics -- The first law of thermodynamics (or law of conservation of energy) states that energy can be neither created nor destroyed but can be converted from one form into another. During any physical or chemical reaction the energy form may be changed but the energy output must equal the energy input. The amount of energy gained or lost by an abiotic or biotic system must equal the amount of energy gained or lost by its surroundings. Stated in another fashion, a major implication of the first law of thermodynamics is that "we can't get anything for nothing or there is no free lunch."

b. Second Law of Thermodynamics -- The second law of thermodynamics explains what happens to energy when it is used (i.e., either converted from one form into another or transferred from one system to another). The second law states that when energy is used it is degraded into a lower quality and less useful form, usually low temperature heat, that is dissipated or dispersed into the surrounding environment. When high-quality energy (i.e., concentrated energy with a great potential for doing useful work) is used to perform work some of it will be degraded to low-quality energy or waste heat which has little potential for performing useful work. No conversion of energy into another form or transfer of energy from one system to another is thus 100% efficient. Stated in colloquial terms, the second law of thermodynamics implies that "we can never break even." Since energy and matter spontaneously flow from areas of high free energy (less disorder or entropy) to areas of low free energy (greater disorder or entropy) the second law of thermodynamics may be interpreted as stating that all systems tend toward a greater state of disorder or entropy. Living organisms and ecosystems, however, are highly ordered systems and would initially appear to be glaring contradictions of the second law. To maintain order living organisms must continually replenish high-quality energy from their environment. Use of this high-quality energy to maintain order in living organisms and ecosystems results in its degradation and return of low-quality energy or waste heat into the surroundings. Unlike nutrients, energy does not cycle within systems but flows through them, is degraded to less useful forms, and must be continually replenished to maintain order. Living organisms, ecosystems, or any economic activity must continually be replenished with high-quality energy that is then inevitably degraded to low-quality energy and is dispersed or dissipated into the surrounding environment thereby increasing its entropy. Advanced industrial societies thus have a great capacity for adding more entropy to the environment.

(3) Trophic Levels

Organisms in ecosystems can be classified by the way in which they obtain energy. Some organisms such as green plants and blue-green algae are capable of producing their own food and are hence called producers or autotrophs. Most organisms are consumers and must feed on other organisms to obtain energy, they are thus also referred to as heterotrophs. Where organisms obtain their energy depends on their trophic level (i.e., feeding level or position along a food chain). Producers support virtually all other living organisms by converting solar energy into chemical energy utilizing photosynthesis. The conversion of radiant energy from the sun into chemical energy by producers can be summarized as:

carbon + water $\xrightarrow[\text{(673 kilocalories)}\nearrow]{\text{solar radiation}\searrow}$ glucose + oxygen + water
dioxide

$$6\ CO_2\ +\ 12\ H_2O\ \xrightarrow[\text{(673 kilocalories)}\nearrow]{\text{solar radiation}\searrow}\ C_6H_{12}O_6\ +\ 6\ O_2\ +\ 6\ H_2O$$

The glucose molecules are converted into more complex sugars, fats, proteins, and starches by plants (producers) and by animals eating plants. Plants and heterotrophs extract energy for their metabolic activity from the food they have produced or obtained utilizing cellular respiration which can be summarized as follows:

glucose + oxygen + water $\xrightarrow{\text{energy}\nearrow}$ carbon + water
dioxide

$$C_6H_{12}O_6\ +\ 6\ H_2O\ +\ 6\ H_2O\ \xrightarrow{\text{energy}\nearrow}\ 6\ CO_2\ +\ 12\ H_2O$$

It should be noted that at each stage of energy transformation or transferal some will be degraded in accordance with the second law of thermodynamics.

Consumers that obtain their food and energy from plants are known as herbivores. Herbivores are eaten by primary carnivores who are in turn eaten by a secondary carnivore. A food chain refers to a sequence of organisms each at a different trophic level feeding on the preceding trophic level (e.g., pine--→pine bark beetle--→woodpecker--→hawk). In nature, most herbivores feed on a variety of different plant species just as carnivores feed on a number of different types of animal species depending on their trophic level. The result is a series of complex interconnected food chains referred to as food webs which give a more complete picture of feeding relationships and energy flows within ecosystems.

Data from terrestrial and aquatic ecosystems indicate only 0.1% to 1.6% of the total incident solar radiation is captured by plants (producers) (Kormondy, 1976). However, photosynthesis only utilizes solar radiation within the wavelength range of 0.4 μm to 0.7 μm or about 40% - 50% of the total energy in the solar spectrum (Rosenberg, 1974). If only photosynthetically active radiation is considered, the efficiency of energy capture by plants would increase to 2% to 6%.

Approximately 50% of the energy fixed by producers is released during plant respiration and dissipates into the environment as heat. An additional 40% of the energy plants capture from the sun remains as uneaten biomass and is eventually decomposed by detritivores. Thus only about 10% of the energy fixed by plants is available to other trophic levels. Herbivores and carnivores assimilate approximately 20% - 60% and 50% - 90%, respectively, of what they eat (Whittaker, 1975). Moreover, animals typically respire at least 50% of the energy they assimilate. The average gross growth efficiency (new protoplasm in growth and reproduction divided by food consumed) is about 10% but may be up to 20% for top carnivores (Westman, 1985).

The loss of energy during the transfer of food results in a decline of net annual production (gross annual production of biomass minus annual respiration) at higher trophic levels (Figure II.2a). Typically, biomass and number of individuals also declines at higher trophic levels (Figure II.2b,c) although this may not always be the case (e.g., many herbivorous insects feeding on a single plant may result in an inverted pyramid) (Westman, 1985). Since an inevitable consequence of the laws of thermodynamics is that energy is dissipated as heat during its exchange the pyramid of productivity (Figure II.2a) is never inverted. There are a number of implications resulting from these energy limitations. First, the number of trophic levels in ecosystems is limited (generally no more than four) by energy constraints. Second, any adverse impact to the plant community will ultimately have negative repercussions for organisms throughout the food web. Third, since organisms near the top of the food chain have low productivities their numbers will generally be small relative to other trophic levels thus making them more vulnerable to extinction.

(4) Productivity of Ecosystems

Since the amount of solar energy fixed by plants ultimately affects how much energy is available to the other trophic levels, the measurement of plant productivity provides a good indicator for overall productivity of the ecosystem. Primary productivity (or producer productivity) of a region is largely a function of climate, with annual precipitation and temperature the most influential climatic variables. However, soil nutrient status, micro-habitat differences, and the effects of periodic disturbance also play important secondary roles. Gross primary productivity (GPP) is the total solar energy fixed or organic matter created by photosynthesis. Net primary productivity (NPP) is the amount of energy or organic matter remaining after plant respiration; it is most often expressed in units of dry organic matter (i.e., $g\ m^{-2}\ yr^{-1}$). Only NPP is available to higher trophic levels and detritivores.

Ecologists often group terrestrial ecosystems with similar vegetation structure or physiognomy into biomes. There are six broad physiognomic groups: forests, woodlands (tree density lower than in forests), shrublands, grasslands, semidesert scrub (less shrub cover than shrublands), and deserts (plant cover often

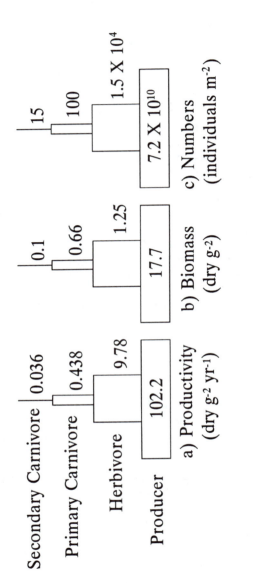

FIGURE II.2

Productivity, biomass, and number pyramids
for an experimental pond

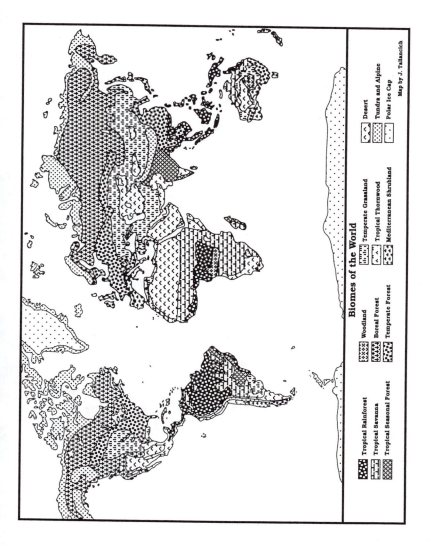

FIGURE II.3

less than 10%) (Whittaker, 1975). The same physiognomic group may be found at different latitudes and in different climates. Specific biome-types may be distinguished such as tropical rainforests, temperate deciduous forests, and boreal forests all of which are dominated by trees. In contrast, alpine meadows, temperate grasslands, and tropical savannas are dominated by grasses. Figure II.3 depicts the distribution of the world's major biomes and Table II.1 lists estimated NPP for selected biomes.

Table II.1 Mean Net Primary Productivity of the Earth's
Major Biomes (g m^{-2} yr^{-1})

Tropical Rainforests	2000
Swamps and Marshes	2000
Temperate Forests	1250
Tropical Savanna	900
Boreal Forests	800
Woodlands and Shrublands	700
Agricultural Lands	650
Temperate Grassland	600
Tundra	140
Desert	40

As noted in Table II.1 the humid tropics with abundant rainfall, intense solar radiation, and warm temperatures exhibit among the world's highest productivities. The longer nights and cooler temperatures in temperate and arctic regions dramatically curtails productivity. For any given latitude where temperature and daylength vary little from region to region NPP is most highly correlated with annual precipitation.

CYCLING OF MATTER

(1) Hydrologic Cycle

The distribution of the world's biomes is best correlated with mean annual precipitation and temperature both of which are largely a function of climate. The hydrologic cycle represents the interchange of water from the oceans, terrestrial systems, and the atmosphere. The essence of the cycle is that water evaporates from the oceans, is transported by wind and is subsequently deposited on land (the form is temperature dependent) where most of it (77%) flows via streams and rivers back to the oceans. The oceans contain 97.2% of the earth's water, ice sheets contain another 2%, and fresh water streams, lakes, and aquifers make up the rest. The amount of fresh water available to living organisms is thus quite small, less than 1% of the earth's total supply of water. While mean annual precipitation is highly correlated with the distribution of biomes, precipitation effectiveness is also important. Precipitation effectiveness refers to the water that is actually available to plants and is largely dependent on seasonality of precipitation, precipitation intensity, precipitation type, and soil condition. A mean annual precipitation of 70 - 80 cm yr^1 (approximately 27 - 31 inches yr^{-1}) can support a relatively lush deciduous forest or a drought adapted shrubland depending whether the precipitation is distributed relatively equally throughout the year or is concentrated over a 4 to 5 month period. Similarly, if precipitation is primarily in the form of snow and not available to plants until snowmelt occurs the vegetation type would be different than if the precipitation was rain. Moreover, if precipitation is intense as in a violent thunderstorm or if the soil is saturated from a previous rainfall, runoff will exceed infiltration and the precipitation event will be of little consequence to plant life.

(2) Biogeochemical Cycles

Of the 92 stable elements on the planet only 17 are essential to all plants and an additional 10 or more are required by other organisms usually in trace quantities. These elements known collectively as essential elements (or nutrients) are required either in large quantities (i.e., macronutrients) or in small or trace quantities (i.e., micronutrients). Examples of macronutrients include: carbon (C), hydrogen (H), nitrogen (N), oxygen (O), phosphorous (P), and sulfur (S) which collectively make up 95% of the biomass of most living organisms. In contrast to energy, nutrients are cycled between the biotic and abiotic systems thus linking them together into functional dynamic ecosystems. Knowledge of these cycles is critical in any prediction or assessment of anthropogenic disruption whether it be a loss of nutrients from increased soil erosion or an addition to a given nutrient budget resulting in eutrophication in the case of phosphorous and potential global warming in the case of carbon.

Nutrient cycling can be classified by whether it occurs within an ecosystem (intrasystem cycling) or whether nutrients are moving in and out of the same ecosystem (intersystem cycling). Intrasystem cycling is a homeostatic mechanism whereby a pool or source of exchangeable nutrients in the form of dead or living biomass is available to plants by continual decomposition and subsequent nutrient uptake. The cycling of nutrients within ecosystems is typically ten times more rapid than intersystem cycling (Barbour *et al.*, 1987). Nutrient cycles are also classified by the location of the major available pool of an essential element. Elements for which the atmosphere is the major reservoir such as carbon and nitrogen have gaseous cycles while phosphorous and sulfur which are found primarily in the earth's crust have sedimentary cycles.

a. Carbon Cycle -- A brief reexamination of the formulas for photosynthesis will reveal the importance of carbon for the earth's living organisms. Indeed, 49% of the dry weight of living organisms is carbon. Carbon has been described as the building block of life because of the nature of its bonding with other elements and because carbon bonds are effective at storing energy. The energy captured by plants during photosynthesis, which ultimately is the energy available to virtually all other organisms including humans, is stored as chemical energy in the carbon bonds of carbohydrate molecules.

Carbon in the atmosphere is available primarily as CO_2 and is removed by plants via photosynthesis and returned to the atmosphere by plant and animal respiration. While the amount of carbon in the troposphere in the form of CO_2 (0.036% or 360 ppm) is small compared to nitrogen (78%) and oxygen (21%) its influence on life is considerable even beyond its role in the critical processes of photosynthesis and respiration. The absorption spectrum of CO_2, from 2 μm to 15 μm, makes it an effective trap of infrared radiation (heat) which the earth radiates with the wavelength of maximum emission at about 10 μm (Rosenberg, 1974). Carbon dioxide is thus also critical in maintaining the earth's heat balance by trapping infrared radiation that would otherwise escape into space. The overall effect is very important considering that an atmosphere without CO_2 would result in an mean global temperature of -17.8°C (0° F) versus the present mean global temperature of 15°C (59° F).

Figure II.4 illustrates the role of living organisms and the oceans in regulating the carbon balance of the planet. Living organisms are both a source and sink of CO_2; however, photosynthesis is a net sink removing more CO_2 from the atmosphere, and storing it as plant biomass, than is replaced by plant and animal respiration. In marine ecosystems CO_2 is removed from the atmosphere by photosynthesizing marine organisms, by dissolving CO_2 in ocean water, and by organisms that take up dissolved CO_2 or CO_3^{2-} (carbonate ions) and HCO_3^- (bicarbonate ions) and use them to build shells and skeletal tissue. When these latter organisms die their shells and skeletons eventually become buried in the ocean sediments. The amount of carbon stored in the sediments of the oceans is 10,000 times that of the total mass of living organism but it is recycled to the atmosphere very slowly often requiring geological processes. Carbon dioxide is, however, released as ocean water warms because cooler water can hold more dissolved gases than warmer water.

A major contemporary concern is the potential for global warming as a result of increased levels of CO_2 and other greenhouse gases in the atmosphere.

Human activities are increasing CO_2 levels in the atmosphere by increasing a source (burning fossil fuels at greater rates) and by destroying sinks through deforestation. The world's forests are currently being cut at an annual rate of 0.8% or by 15.4 million ha per year (38.05 million acres or an area the size of the state of Washington) (Aldous, 1993). A recent consensus reached by the scientific community noted that given the current rates of fossil fuel burning and deforestation, the levels of CO_2 in the atmosphere will be twice the pre-industrial levels sometime by the middle of the next century resulting in 1.5° C - 4.5° C (or a 2.5° C "best estimate") increase in global temperature (Kerr, 1990). Ecological and economic consequences of such temperature shifts would be tremendous as global climate and vegetational zones would shift northward (and southward in the southern hemisphere).

b. Nitrogen Cycle -- Living organisms require nitrogen for the production of amino acids, proteins, DNA (deoxyribonucleic acid), and RNA (ribonucleic acid). While nitrogen gas (N_2) comprises 78% of the air in the troposphere it cannot be utilized by plants and animals in this form. The chemical breakdown and cycling of nitrogen is mediated by several species of bacteria. Any alteration of the soil that deleteriously affects these bacteria (including increased soil acidification) may thus directly affect nitrogen cycling. Moreover, nitrogen typically is the limiting soil nutrient in terrestrial ecosystems since the amount available in soil is small relative to the amount withdrawn by plants.

The conversion of N_2 in the troposphere into nitrates (NO_3^-) is called nitrogen fixation (Figure II.5). Cyanobacteria in the soil and *Rhyzobium* bacteria which are mutualistically associated with the roots of legume species (pea family) and a few other non-leguminous plant species are largely responsible for the fixing of tropospheric N_2 into forms that are readily available to plants. Organisms on higher trophic levels ultimately derive their nitrogen from plants. The organic nitrogen in dead biomass is converted into ammonia (NH_3) by bacteria in a process known as ammonification. Nitrification is the process by which NH_3 is converted into NO_2^- and subsequently to NO_3^-. Nitrates that are not utilized by plants may eventually be converted to N_2 as a result of another bacteria mediated processes called denitrification and ultimately make their way back into the atmosphere. Another byproduct of denitrification is nitrous oxide (N_2O) which when released into the atmosphere acts as both a greenhouse gas and an ozone layer depleting gas. Overfertilization of agricultural fields with nitrate fertilizers may release relatively large amounts of N_2O as surplus NO_3^- is denitrified. In addition, NO_3^- is readily leached from the soil into surface and groundwater drinking supplies where it can become a carcinogenic pollutant.

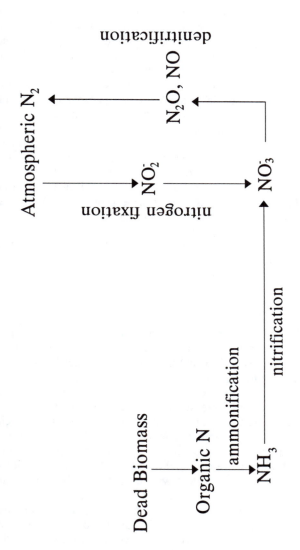

FIGURE II.5 Simplified nitrogen cycle

c. Phosphorous Cycle -- Phosphorous is second only to nitrogen as the most critical soil nutrient for plants. Living organisms require phosphorous for DNA and RNA formation, energy transfer during respiration, and for bone and teeth formation. In addition, plants require phosphorous for flowering and fruit formation. Phosphorous is mostly present in the earth's crust in an inorganic and insoluble form which is not available to plants. Only about 1% of the phosphorous in the earth's crust is available to plants. As phosphate containing rock deposits and fossils are slowly weathered phosphorous is dissolved in soil water and taken up by plants. Animals ultimately get their phosphorous from plants. The phosphorous in animal wastes and in dead plant and animal biomass is returned to the soil where much of it leaches into streams and rivers and eventually makes its way into the ocean. There is thus a net flow of phosphorous from terrestrial ecosystems to marine systems. Some phosphorous in marine ecosystems is returned to land as the wastes of marine birds (guano) such as pelicans and cormorants. Unlike carbon and nitrogen, the levels of phosphorous in terrestrial systems are decreasing due to the net flow into the oceans. Mining of large quantities of phosphate rock for the production of phosphorous fertilizers and detergents only exacerbates this loss.

LIMITING FACTORS

The growth and distribution of living organisms are constrained by resource availability in the physical (i.e., abiotic) environment. Such constraints are typically known as limiting factors and can affect the growth and distribution of living organisms by being present in quantities which are either too great or insufficient. The effects of limiting factors on a population of a species is depicted by tolerance ranges. Figure II.6 illustrates the optimal range of mean annual precipitation for a particular species as well as the upper and lower lethal limits. This species is optimally adapted to regions which have 80 cm to 100 cm (approximately 32 to 40 inches) of precipitation annually. In addition, individuals of this population cannot survive in regions with mean annual precipitation rates of less than 60 cm (24 inches) or more than 120 cm (48 inches). On a regional scale, climate and soil are the limiting factors with the largest influence on the growth and distribution of organisms. In some areas, however, anthropogenic disturbance (e.g., pollution, habitat destruction, etc.) may also play an important role. Since climate and soil affect plant productivity and the eventual endpoint of successional processes, they also play important indirect and direct roles in the overall assimilative capacity of an area.

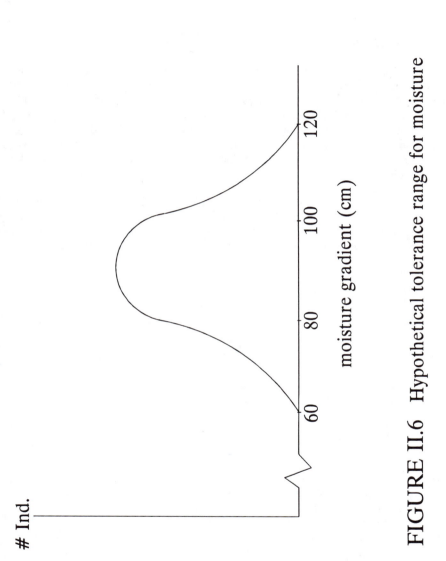

FIGURE II.6   Hypothetical tolerance range for moisture

(1) Climate

Climate can limit the growth and distribution of organisms by providing insufficient quantities of a particular physical factor (e.g., insufficient heat or precipitation) or too much of some factor (e.g., too much heat or precipitation). While there is significant spatial and temporal variation in climatic elements they are influenced by a few climatic controls. On a regional basis and over the long-term the complex interactions in the atmosphere which in turn limit the growth and distribution of organisms within that region are largely determined by the factors discussed below.

a. Solar Radiation -- Incoming solar radiation is electromagnetic radiation, has wavelengths of approximately 0.1 μm - 2.5 μm, and falls in the middle of the electromagnetic spectrum.   The electromagnetic spectrum (Table II.2) characterizes radiation by its wavelength. High energy radiation has short

Table II.2 The Electromagnetic Spectrum

Type of Radiation	Approximate Wavelengths (μm)
Gamma Rays	10^{-7} - 10^{-4}
X Rays	10^{-8} - 10^{-2}
Ultraviolet	10^{-4} - 10^{-1}
Visible	0.4 - 0.7
Infrared	7.6×10^{-1} - 3.0×10^3
Radio Waves	3.0×10^3 - 3.0×10^{10}
Electric Waves	3.0×10^{10} - ∞

wavelengths while low energy radiation has longer wavelengths. Three types of radiation are particularly important to humans and other living organisms, these will be discussed in turn.

Ultra-violet (UV) radiation (see Table II.2) is harmful to living organisms but is largely screened by the ozone (O_3) layer in the lower stratosphere. Were it not for the existence of the O_3-layer the levels of UV radiation reaching the earth's surface would be lethal to living organisms.   Indeed, prior to the formation of this protective layer life only existed in the oceans where UV radiation was sufficiently screened. The full development of the O_3-layer (a process which took almost 2 billion years) allowed the eventual colonization of terrestrial systems by living organisms approximately 400 to 450 million years ago. Since the O_3-layer does not screen all incoming UV radiation some living organisms, including humans, are still vulnerable to UV radiation exposure. The visible portion of the electromagnetic spectrum (see Table II.2) contains the wavelengths that can be detected by human eyes. The shorter wavelengths are seen as the colors violet and blue while the longer wavelengths are seen as red. Infrared radiation with wavelengths of 0.7 μm to 3000 μm is heat and is considered longwave radiation.

Not all of the solar radiation incident on the atmosphere is absorbed by the earths's surface. Approximately 25% of total insolation is reflected back into space by the atmosphere's albedo (reflectivity). Another 8% is reflected by the earth's surface, thus 33% of the incoming solar radiation is reflected back to space. Twenty two percent of total insolation is absorbed by the atmosphere leaving 45% to be actually absorbed by the earth's surface. Approximately 75% of the solar radiation absorbed by the earth's surface falls on the oceans and drives the hydrologic cycle. As the earth's surface and the atmosphere are warmed by incoming solar radiation they heat up and subsequently reradiate infrared radiation. Most of this reradiated infrared radiation (69%) is ultimately emitted directly into space. Thirty-nine percent is trapped in the atmosphere by heat trapping gases such as H_2O, CO_2, and other greenhouse gases and subsequently reradiated back to the surface. The term "greenhouse effect" thus refers to the continual reradiation of infrared radiation between the earth's surface and atmosphere.

b. Latitude -- Latitude, or the degree to which an area is located north or south of the equator, affects climate through its effect on the intensity of solar radiation (amount of energy per unit land area) reaching the surface. Because the earth's surface is curved, solar radiation is intercepted by the surface in a more or less perpendicular fashion (high incident angle) at the equator and at a lesser incident angle further north or south of the equator. The lower the angle of incidence the greater the diffusion of solar energy over the earth's surface. In contrast, a high angle of incidence (near 90°) concentrates more solar energy over a smaller surface area. The net result of this differential heating of the earth's surface is the development of a heat surplus at equatorial regions and a heat deficit at higher latitudes. Since the atmosphere acts like a system and attempts to more equally distribute heat energy there is a net flow of heat from lower latitudes to higher latitudes giving rise to a series of circulation cells collectively known as the global circulation system. Similarly, the differential heating of the oceans gives rise to warm currents that transport heat to higher latitudes from equatorial regions and cold currents that bring colder water from polar regions to lower latitudes.

c. Rotation of the Planet -- Air masses move along the earth's surface from areas of high pressure (descending air) to areas of low pressure (ascending air). However, these wind patterns are deflected from their normal path of travel by the rotation of the earth; this deflection is known as the coriolis effect. In the northern hemisphere the deflection is clockwise or to the right of the normal path while in the southern hemisphere it is counterclockwise or to the left of the normal path of travel. The coriolis effect gives rise to such commonly known wind patterns as the westerlies and the trade wind belts. In addition, the earth's rotation affects ocean currents and storm systems such as hurricanes in a similar fashion.

d. Altitude -- As air rises it cools at a fairly constant rate (dry adiabatic lapse rate) of approximately 10° C per 1000 m (5.5° F per 1000 ft). As the air cools its ability to hold moisture decreases and with continual cooling the air parcel may reach the dew point (the temperature at which it is saturated with water vapor and condensation begins). If the air mass continues to rise and cool, condensation will release the latent heat of condensation causing the rate of cooling with increasing altitude to decrease (wet adiabatic lapse rate) to approximately 6.5° C per 1000 m (2° F per 1000 ft). In contrast, as an air parcel descends in altitude it undergoes adiabatic warming at the dry adiabatic lapse rate.

e. Topography -- The climatic changes that occur as a result of increasing elevation in a mountain range coincide roughly with climatic changes that occur with increasing latitude (i.e., moving further north or south from the equator). Mountains may also act to block or divert winds and other meteorological phenomenon. Moreover, the location of a region with respect to the windward or exposed side and the leeward or sheltered side of a mountain range can dramatically affect climate. As moist air approaches a mountain range and is forced over the range the air mass will cool adiabatically. Since cool air has a lower moisture holding capacity much of the moisture will condense and drop out as precipitation on the windward side, the form (i.e., rain, snow, or sleet) is temperature dependent. As the now dry air mass proceeds over the mountain range and down the leeward side it will warm adiabatically thus producing a generally arid or desert climate type. This phenomena is know as the rainshadow effect and is responsible for the largely desert areas of eastern Washington, Oregon, and California.

f. Oceans -- Since water heats and cools more slowly than land maritime regions typically experience milder winters and summers than continental regions. Ocean currents also have a profound effect on regional climatic patterns. The warm Gulf Stream/North Atlantic current that transports heat from subtropical regions northward has a modifying effect on the climate of western Europe. In contrast, the cold California current off the west coast of the United States is responsible for the arid like climates of southern California (essentially San Francisco and south) and Baja, Mexico. As warm moist Pacific air approaches the west coast it travels over the cold California current, is cooled, and subsequently loses much of its moisture before reaching the coast.

(2) Soil

Soil provides a number of important ecological functions: 1) it provides physical support primarily for plants but also for a variety of soil dwelling organisms; 2) in most ecosystems it is the major pool of nutrients (the major exception is tropical rainforests where the living biomass is the major nutrient pool and the soils are relatively depauperate in nutrients) and is thus critical for nutrient storage; 3) it is critical for water storage, since plants generally lose water to the air even in very humid conditions, the soil is their source of water; and 4) it continually supplies nutrients from the breakdown of rock, soil particles, and the organic layer (humus) which largely consists of partially decomposed organic material.

The material from which soil is formed is known as parent material (PM) which is usually some type of rock. The PM is eventually broken down by a series of weathering processes. Physical weathering such as thermal expansion and contraction and freeze-thaw action can cause rock to break down into smaller fragments. Rainfall, which is a weak acid (average pH of 5.6) as a result of combining with CO_2 in the atmosphere to form carbonic acid (H_2CO_3), acts as a chemical weathering agent. Living organisms also contribute to the weathering process through the action of bacteria and/or lichens breaking down rock surfaces or through the action of plant roots. The soil type that eventually develops is primarily a function of the original PM and the climate of the region.

Mature soils have a series of layers (soil horizons) which vary depending on the soil type. The top layer is the O-horizon or litter layer and consists of newly deposited plant and animal material, fungi, and other organic matter. The first true soil layer is the A-horizon which is covered by the organic layer and typically contains a large proportion of soil nutrients. The B-horizon contains mostly inorganic material and the C-horizon consists of partially weathered PM. Particle size distribution is another important characteristic affecting soil type. The most important soil particles consist of clays (less than 0.002 mm in diameter), silt (0.002 mm to 0.05 mm in diameter), and sand (0.05 mm to 2.0 mm in diameter) (these size classes are based on United States Department of Agriculture standards; the reader should note that other standards vary the size class distributions slightly). The soil texture class can be discerned from the relative amounts of these three particles utilizing a soil texture triangle (Figure II.7). Soils with roughly equal proportions of these particle sizes are called loams and are typically the most ideal for plant growth. The organic layer and the clay content are the major source of nutrients available to plants. Clay also increases a soil's water holding capacity while sand increases soil permeability, or the rate with which water travels through the soil.

Since the large proportion of nutrients are in the top few centimeters of a soil (i.e., topsoil) the erosion of this layer, even partially, can dramatically reduce the productivity of the system. According to the U.S. Soil Conservation Service approximately 1.2 million hectares (3 million acres) of productive soils are lost each year in the U.S. from erosion and other anthropogenic activities. One reason that soil erosion has not received the high priority and attention it deserves may be due to the seemingly low average rate of erosion in any one specific area. On average 1 mm (0.04 inches) of topsoil is lost in an area over the course of a year, hardly a rate most people would notice. However, consider that over the course of 25 years that same area would on average lose 25 mm (1 inch) of soil, an amount it requires nature 500 years or more to replace.

BIOTIC INTERACTIONS AS LIMITING FACTORS

While physical limiting factors such as climatic variables (e.g., temperature, precipitation, etc.) and soils may impose limits on the growth and distribution of populations of species the effects of biotic interactions impose additional limitations and must therefore be superimposed on the purely physical constraints. It is initially important to distinguish between two ecologically important features of a species, the habitat and the niche. The habitat of species is the general physical environment in which the species is found (e.g., a forest habitat, an aquatic habitat, a prairie habitat, etc.). The niche is all encompassing and includes every aspect, resource requirement, and biotic interaction of the species. As such the niche includes the habitat (i.e., abiotic environment) and can in general terms be defined as the unique position of a species in an ecosystem. Since the niche of every species is unique, no two species can have the same niche and live in the same ecosystem. This principle, known as the competitive exclusion principle, means that if two species occupy the same niche in the same ecosystem the overlap of their resource requirements will be so complete that the resulting intense competition will cause one species to eventually become extinct. The actual habitat and niche (realized niche) of species are primarily determined by interactions with other species and the physical environment.

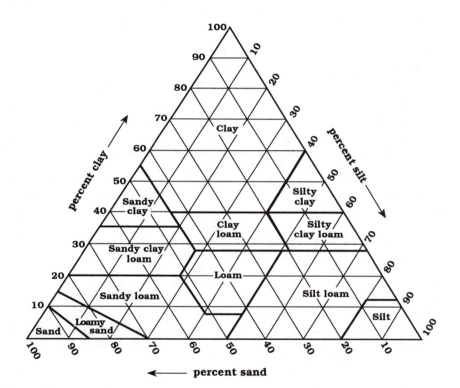

FIGURE II.7

(1) Population Growth

The growth of populations of species are greatly influenced by resource limitations and the number of organisms that are present at any given time.

a. Exponential Growth -- If resources are not limiting populations will grow at an ever increasing rate resulting in a J-shaped growth curve characteristic of exponential growth (Figure II.8a). The instantaneous rate of growth can be characterized by the following differential equation: $dN/dt = rN_t$; where dN/dt is the rate of growth or number of individuals added per unit time, r is the intrinsic rate of increase, and N_t is the number of individuals present at time t. Since both sides of the equality are positive an increase on one side causes an increase on the other. As the number of individuals present increases the rate of growth increases or more simply put the larger the population the faster it is growing. Exponential growth is thus an example of a positive feedback system where the number of individuals and the growth rate interact in a positive or reinforcing manner.

b. Logistic Growth -- In nature populations cannot, of course, continually grow in an exponential fashion. Limited resources put a constraint on population growth and size. The maximum number of individuals of a population for which a system can provide resources is known as the carrying capacity. The presence of a carrying capacity results in an S-shaped or sigmoid population growth curve characteristic of logistic growth (Figure II.8b). As with exponential growth, the instantaneous growth rate for logistic growth can be depicted by a differential equation: $dN/dt = rN_t(K-N_t/K)$ where K is the carrying capacity and all other variables are as described for exponential growth. The term in the parenthesis is crucial in explaining a major feature of logistic growth. If N_t is less than K (i.e., the number of individuals present is less than the maximum for which the system can provide resources) then $K-N_t$ is positive, the growth rate is positive, and the population will continue to grow. If, however, the population has exceeded its carrying capacity resulting in N_t being greater than K, then $K-N_t$ will be negative, the growth rate will be negative, and the population will decline to below the carrying capacity. Logistic growth is thus an example of a negative feedback system where the carrying capacity (or resource limitations) cause a reversal of population growth until the population size falls within the constraints of resource availability. The difference in the number of individuals expected from exponential growth and those actually accommodated by the carrying capacity is sometimes known as the environmental resistance or the number of individuals that did not get added to the population because of limiting factors. The differential equation for logistic growth will not, when plotted, result in a

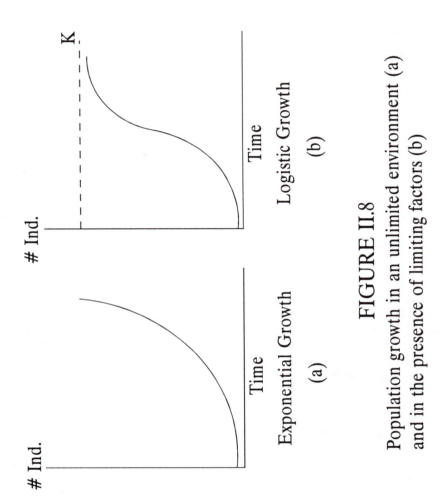

FIGURE II.8

Population growth in an unlimited environment (a)
and in the presence of limiting factors (b)

sigmoid curve but a parabola indicating that as N_t approaches K, rN_t approaches zero and population growth ceases. It is the integral form of the equation (N_t = $K/1+e^{-rt}$) that yields a sigmoid growth curve characteristic of logistic growth and depicted in Figure II.8b.

The carrying capacity of a population is not static but may increase or decrease depending on abiotic and biotic limiting factors. A drought or unseasonably freezing temperatures may, for example, reduce the carrying capacity for herbivores by destroying producer populations. Anthropogenic activities such as pollution or habitat destruction may also reduce the carrying capacity for populations of plant species. The effect may be magnified as the carrying capacities of herbivores and ultimately carnivores would also be reduced. It is interesting to consider that humans are the only species capable of altering their carrying capacity. They are able to increase their carrying capacity through technological innovations, yet ironically that same technology can create unwanted side effects such as toxic wastes and air and water pollution which in turn can decrease the carrying capacity of some regions.

(2) Competition

Competition is a mutually adverse interaction between organisms utilizing a common resource. Since the competing organisms utilize the same resource they must to some extent have overlapping niches. Intraspecific competition is thus greater than interspecific competition since niche overlap is greater. Recall the differential equations for exponential growth and logistic growth (i.e., dN/dt = rN_t and dN/dt = $rN_t(K-N_t/K)$). By rearranging the terms in the logistic equation (dN/dt = rN_t-rN^2/K) it becomes clear that rN^2/K is the decline in population growth due to overcrowding or intraspecific competition for scarce resources.

During interspecific competition natural selection drives organisms to partition resources and hence reduce competition. It can thus alter the range over which species are able to extract resources. Figure II.9a depicts the tolerance ranges of two hypothetical species, A and B, each of which are optimally adapted for extracting resources at points X and Z, respectively. The zone of overlap (shaded portion), near point Y, is where the two species will compete for the same resources; however, neither is particularly well suited to extract resources from this portion of the environmental gradient. Suppose a third species, C, optimally adapted for resource utilization at point Y enters the system (Figure II.9b). The degree of resource utilization overlap (shaded portion) and competition is now much larger. Because competition is a mutually adverse interaction that requires an expenditure of energy normally used for food gathering, reproduction, and other life functions, natural selection over time tends

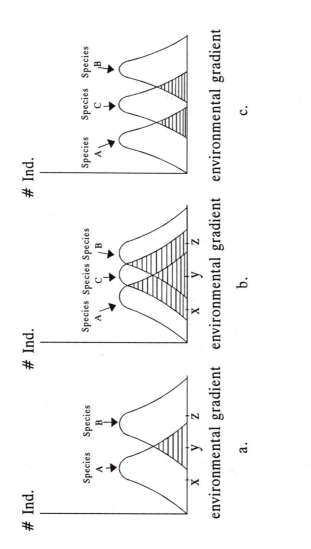

FIGURE II.9   Competition along a hypothetical
environmental gradient

to minimize competition. The net result is a narrowing of each species' tolerance range (Figure II.9c) as they accommodate one another and a concomitant reduction in the region along the environmental gradient that each extracts resources. Competition can thus reduce the physiological range of a species (range to which a species is physiologically adapted) to that found in nature or to its ecological range (actual range due to competitive effects). A classic example of this phenomena is exotic ornamental plant species which grow quite well in gardens and manicured lawns where they are not competing with native plant species. These exotic species are, however, rarely found growing in more natural environments where they would have to compete with successful native species.

(3) Predation

Predation is the process by which a predator uses another live organism as an energy source and thus removes the prey from its population (Colinvaux, 1986). The most common assumption about predator-prey relationships is that they consist of some variation of a set of coupled oscillations where both predator and prey populations fluctuate together. Some of the simplest predator-prey coupled oscillations are derived from the differential Lotka-Volterra equations where the number of prey organisms removed is directly related to the product of the prey and predator populations (Ricklefs, 1990). Such oscillations have been achieved under laboratory conditions with micro-organisms and have been reported in simple systems such as arctic environments with few species.

Predators of large prey animals "act primarily as a check on fecundity" (Colinvaux, 1986). These predators kill primarily the old and sick prey individuals, those which would eventually be part of the natural mortality rate. The number of these predators is largely determined by the number of sick and old prey which is, of course, directly affected by predation on the young (Colinvaux, 1986). Unless the predator population is too dense or prey populations are depressed for other reasons, predators do not normally attack animals in their prime. Even if prey populations are low the effect of predation is usually minimal if prey density is also low. Prey defenses are also an important factor in determining the effect of predation. Large size or poisonous secretions while simple defenses are usually quite effective. More generalized predators often react to density dependent factors so that the most common prey species becomes the one of choice. Colinvaux (1986:238-239) notes that the importance of predation as a regulator of prey populations depends on: "1) ability of prey to defend itself; 2) ability of prey to escape detection; 3) prey densities obtainable in the absence of predators (potential of prey as food); 4) prey dispersal in the absence of predators; ....5) attack properties of the predator; 6) numerical response of the predator (a function of fecundity);"...and "7) functional responses of the predator."

(4) Other Interactions

There are a number of other interactions between species that are also of ecological significance. An all inclusive list and description of these interactions will not be attempted here, rather those interactions whose disruption by anthropogenic disturbance would likely have a significant ecological and subsequent economic cost will be addressed.

a. Mutualism -- Mutualism or true symbiosis is an obligatory interaction between two species where the absence of the interaction depresses the growth of both species. A common example is pollination, a mutualistic interaction between pollinators and flowering plants. The costs to agriculture alone that would accrue if the populations of pollination vectors were suddenly destroyed or depressed would surely run into the billions. Symbiotic nitrogen fixation, an interaction between *Rhizobium* bacteria and legumes described in the nitrogen cycle, is also extremely valuable to agriculture and natural ecosystems. Of critical importance in plant communities with respect to nutrient uptake are mycorrhizal associations. Mycorrhizae (a type of soil fungi) form mutualistic associations with the roots of higher plants. The roots exude amino acids to the mycorrhizae while the fungus aids the plant in nutrient uptake particularly with phosphorous, calcium, and potassium. The result is a stimulation of plant growth between 25% to 300%.

b. Commensalism -- During a commensalistic interaction one species benefits and the effect on the other is neutral. Common examples include epiphytes, such as spanish moss (which is a bromeliad not a moss) growing on oak trees, and vines which use a variety of trees for structural support. A classic case of commensalism is the nurse plant syndrome where larger shrubs or trees "nurse" seedlings of other species protecting them from herbivory, frost damage, and providing shade in the summer. The best demonstrated example of this syndrome is the saguaro cactus of the southwest deserts (primarily the Sonoran Desert in Arizona) whose seedlings are protected by palo verde and some 15 other plant species. The decline of saguaro cacti near Tucson has been hypothesized to be due, at least in part, to the phytotoxic effects of tropospheric O_3 emanating from Tucson on the nurse plants.

c. Amensalism -- Interactions between two species where the growth of one is depressed and the effect on the other is neutral is known as amensalism. These interactions can occur at several levels. At the producer-decomposer level, for example, the plant species which dominate a forest canopy can influence whether bacteria or fungi comprise the dominant decomposers in the soil. In conifer forests fungi dominate the soil because conifer foliage contains tannins which when leached by rain acidify the soil under the canopy. Since bacteria are especially sensitive to increases in acidity fungi tend to dominate conifer forest soils and bacteria tend to dominate the soils of deciduous forests. A special subset of amensalistic interactions, known as allelopathy, involves the release of chemicals by one plant species which will inhibit the growth of other plant species. For example, in Californian shrublands the release of allelochemics by certain shrub species has been shown to inhibit the growth of nearby competing grasses. Moreover, it is common knowledge in the midwest that tomato plants will not grow beneath walnut trees. In this case the chemical juglone is leached from the foliage of walnut trees and makes the soil inhospitable for tomato plants. An important level of amensalism involves producers and herbivores. Many plant species avoid herbivory by invertebrates by producing secondary compounds making them nonpalatable.   In many cases the insect herbivores are able to overcome this evolutionary hurdle by developing resistance mechanisms which in turn act as new selective agents for plants. The insect and plant world are thus locked in an evolutionary chemical war; a major reason why plants are such a rich potential source of chemicals for medicinal and scientific uses.

SPECIES DIVERSITY

(1) Species Richness and Equitability

Species diversity is a concept about which the lay public generally has many misconceptions. Consider for example two forested sites each of which contain only two species, pines and oaks. Suppose further that the number of oaks and pines on each site are distributed in the following manner:

Species	Site 1	Site 2
Pine	90 individuals	50 individuals
Oak	10 individuals	50 individuals

Which site has the greatest species diversity? To answer the question the two components of diversity must be examined. The first is species richness which refers to the number of species per unit area. In the example above both sites contain only two species, species richness is thus equal on the two sites. The second component of diversity is the relative abundance of species at a site, a property known as equitability or evenness. Since site 2 has an equal number of oaks and pines equitability at this site is higher than on site 1. Since richness is the same in the two sites but equitability is greater on site 2, the latter would be considered to have a greater total diversity.

In general, the number of species encountered will increase as the area surveyed increases. Species richness is thus standardized by the use of a fixed sample area and is denoted as number of species per unit area. If two unequally sized areas are to be compared with respect to richness the values must be standardized utilizing formulae usually provided in any standard plant ecology textbook, even then, however, problems persists. It is thus best to compare sites of equal areas.

Equitability or the relative abundance of species ultimately reflects the way in which species have partitioned resources. The term evenness is sometimes used to refer to the evenness of the distribution of resources among the species. Most ecologists, however, use the terms equitability and evenness interchangeably. It should be noted that in the above example the relative abundance of pines and oaks was measured using density. While density can be a useful measure of relative abundance especially when the species compared are relatively equal in size, other measures can provide a clearer picture of relative abundance or resource partitioning. For example, consider a site that contains two large oak trees and 200 small grass individuals. Clearly, density would be an inappropriate measure of relative abundance because the two oaks may be utilizing a disproprotionately greater amount of the available resources than all 200 grass individuals collectively. Other measures of relative abundance include foliar cover (the percent of surface area covered by the foliage of each species), biomass (the dry weight of each species per unit area), or basal area (the sum of the area of the cross sections of all individual trees of a given species). Net primary productivity is also a good measure of relative abundance but it is extremely time consuming to estimate and usually requires destructive sampling techniques.

(2) Heterogeneity Indices

While it is usually better to keep the two components of diversity separate so their independent influence on total diversity can be assessed, there are a number of commonly used indices that combine richness and equitability into a single numerical number Such indices are collectively known as heterogeneity indices. These indices have become increasingly popular in environmental impact assessment and have become quite common in environmental impact statements. It is beyond the scope of this book to analyze and critique all available heterogeneity indices; however, the two most common indices will be briefly addressed.

E.H. Simpson (1949) proposed one of the earliest and one of the simplest heterogeneity indices:

$$C = \Sigma p_i^2$$

where p_i is the proportional abundance of the ith species:

$$p_i = \frac{\text{relative abundance of species i}}{\Sigma(\text{relative abundances of all species})}$$

The index essentially gives the probability that two randomly picked individuals will belong to the same species and ranges from 0 to 1. If a site or system is monospecific (i.e., all individuals belong to one species), C reaches its maximum value of one. It is inversely related to total diversity, the lower its value the greater the diversity. The higher the value the more concentrated the dominance among a few species (Simpson's index is thus also referred to as concentration of dominance). Because of its inverse relationship with diversity several modifications of Simpson's index exist, the most common are 1-C and 1/C. The power function used in Simpson's index causes it to weight the most abundant species. This is an important property to consider if the index is used, for example, to assess the effects of anthropogenic activities on threatened species which will by definition be rare.

The second heterogeneity index that will be discussed is the Shannon-Wiener statistic: $H' = -\Sigma p_i \log p_i$ where p_i is again the proportional abundance of the ith species. This index is also referred to as the Shannon-Weaver index in some texts and the natural logarithm (ln) is sometimes substituted for the base ten logarithm. The Shannon-Wiener index is based on information theory and is a measure of the average uncertainty that a randomly selected individual will belong to a particular species. This index differs from Simpson's index in two fundamental ways. First, H' is not inversely related to diversity and it reaches its minimum value of 0 if only one species is present. The maximum value, for a given species richness, is reached when all species have the same relative abundances. Second, because of the logarithmic nature of the function, H' responds most strongly to rare species. This latter feature is an important consideration if the index is utilized to describe the effects of some anthropogenic disturbance on the dominant or moderately abundant species.

In addition to the problems and constraints afflicting individual heterogeneity indices[1], these type of indices should not be used as a sole criterion of ecological integrity or as a measure of the degree of ecosystem disturbance. A common argument made for continued clearcutting operations in national forests is that species diversity and habitat heterogeneity sometimes increases after such cuts. The clear implication of the argument is that an increase in diversity is in of itself a good thing and thus enhances the ecological integrity of the system. While some of the basis of these arguments may lie in the controversial notion that greater species diversity is associated with increased community stability (see section on stability), other ecological characteristics also have to be examined. For example, removal of the mature forest canopy and the disturbance associated with this type of logging practice allows opportunistic shade intolerant weedy species to invade. Moreover, it can create opportunities for exotic species to become established at the detriment to native species. The subsequent soil erosion and inevitable loss of nutrients following clearcutting, in conjunction with the invasion of disturbance species, may severely hamper the ability of the system to fully recover to one resembling the pre-disturbance state. The increase in diversity observed on these sites is thus not an indication of greater ecological integrity and stability but more likely just the opposite.

The actual use of heterogeneity indices in assessing the effects of pollution and impacts has produced rather interesting results. Jerry Wilm and Troy Dorris (1968) used the Shannon-Wiener index to measure the effects of effluent discharges on aquatic invertebrate communities of streams in Oklahoma. They reported higher H' values downstream from the discharge point than in the upstream control area. Similarly, R. C. Swartz (1980) also used the Shannon-Wiener index (in addition to other indices) to measure the effects of dredging on benthic invertebrate communities and found a higher H' in these communities approximately a month after dredging than prior to disturbance. At face value these studies appear to indicate that dumping pollutant effluents into or dredging aquatic systems increases the diversity of the invertebrate communities and that these activities therefore have some ecologically beneficial effect. Since Swartz (1980) also collected data on species richness and percent abundance the overall effects can be interpreted more clearly. His data indicate that a species moderately abundant prior to dredging was dominant after dredging (increasing from 12.2% to 30.7%) while the pre-dredging dominant decreased from 32.4% to 3.5% after dredging. Thus one invertebrate species was replaced by another as the dominant. In addition, a relatively rare species prior to dredging (abundance of 0.1%) increased to 1.7% after dredging. Since the Shannon-Wiener function is sensitive to changes in rare species this caused a rise in the index above pre-dredge conditions. In summary, heterogeneity indices should be used with caution since they confound the effects of species richness and equitablity. In addition, they should be used in conjunction with other ecological data and information or they should not be used at all (Westman, 1985).

(3) Diversity Gradients

Ecologists have for some time noticed that some areas have more species than others.   These observations have resulted in a number of rather broad generalizations concerning the spatial patterning or gradients of diversity.   These broad diversity gradients are presented with the caveat that exceptions can be found for each due to local climatic patterns and other environmental circumstances. A given unit area of land typically has a greater diversity than the same unit area of ocean. Continental diversity is also generally higher than for an equal area of an island. Diversity also changes with elevation on the slopes of mountains, the lower elevations exhibiting greater diversity than higher elevations.   Perhaps the most important diversity gradient is latitudinal, the general decrease in diversity with distance from the equator. Tropical regions thus exhibit the highest diversity (e.g., tropical rainforests) and polar regions the lowest.

A number of other important characteristics change concomitantly with diversity as the distance from the equator increases.   Tropical regions exhibit more stable physical environments than regions located further north or south (e.g., seasonal variation is less pronounced and daylength remains virtually unchanged near the equator).   Biotic limiting factors or selective pressures, especially competition, predominantly affect resource partitioning, growth, and distribution of organisms in tropical regions. In contrast, abiotic factors (i.e., the physical environment) become more important further north or south of the equator. The two latter trends give rise to differences in the general life history patterns of organisms. The most widely utilized characterization of species' life history patterns is the r- vs. K-selected classification (MacArthur and Wilson, 1967).   The r refers to the intrinsic rate of increase and K refers to the carrying capacity. Species that are r-selected are better adapted to physically harsh (less stable), temporary, or disturbed habitats where a large allocation of energy to reproduction, a low allocation of energy to maintenance and competition, and a short lifespan are adaptive. If for example, a large proportion of a r-selected population is extirpated because of environmental perturbations or disruptions, the high reproductive rate of the survivors would ensure the continuation of the species.   K-selected species allocate less energy to reproduction and more to maintenance and competition and are thus longer lived than r-selected species. This adaptive strategy is advantageous where the physical environment is more stable and competition with other species is more intense.   In general, the proportion of K-selected species decreases and r-selected species increases with distance from the equator. As implied earlier, these are only generalizations and local circumstances can be found to provide exceptions; however, these general trends have helped shape current ecological theory.

SUCCESSION

(1) Successional Concepts

Ecological succession refers to the development of an ecosystem over time in the absence of disturbance or in an interval between disturbances. During the course of succession species composition changes in some predictable and directional manner until a more or less steady-state endpoint or climax is reached. Two broad types of succession are generally recognized, primary and secondary succession. Primary succession occurs on bare sites usually bare rock such as newly formed volcanic extrusions or rock exposed by retreating glaciers. Secondary succession occurs following disturbance such as the gradual replacement of forests following a fire or major storm event such as a hurricane. Successions are further categorized by the processes which drive them. If the biota themselves modify the environment making it more suitable for the next successional stage or seral stage the process is known as autogenic succession. In contrast, allogenic succession refers to forces other than the biota such as climate change or a change in a river meander modifying the environment resulting in a habitat more suitable to the next seral stage or suite of successional species.

The conceptualization of the successional process and climax state has changed dramatically during the twentieth century. Frederick Clements (1916) described succession with such authority that it was not reexamined until almost a half a century later. He viewed plant communities as "superorganisms" which had their own distinct characteristics above and beyond the individual species that comprised the community. The Clementsian view held that for any given climatic region there was a single climax community and all other communities in the region were simply at different stages of development. Clements viewed communities as organisms which developed from infancy to maturity during the successional process. Whole communities would thus replace one another due to autogenic processes until the climatic climax is finally achieved. His notion of seral replacement was both obligatory and slow in its convergence to the steady-state or climax system.

The view that communities act like "superorganisms" has little scientific basis and has largely been discarded (Westman, 1985; Colinvaux, 1986; Barbour et al., 1987). Even during Clements' time, Henry Gleason (1926) argued that plants, like other products of natural selection, each have their own individual adaptations and tolerances. It would, however, take almost fifty years for Gleason's ideas to gain acceptance. The present view of succession is based on the notion of species individuality as proposed by Gleason (1926) and the Russian plant ecologist L.G. Ramensky (1924). Instead of whole communities replacing each other, succession is now viewed as individual plant species replacing each other as the habitat is modified by autogenic and/or allogenic processes. The notion of the climatic climax has also come under considerable scrutiny. While climatic factors are still considered the predominant selective forces, physical features such as soil, slope, aspect, and other microhabitat features are now known to dramatically affect the eventual species composition and diversity of the climax system. More recently, researchers have noted the importance of disturbance and stochastic (random or chance events) factors influencing the outcome of the successional processes or resulting in no stable steady-state endpoint at all.

In contrast to Clements' earlier climatic climax, ecologists now recognize that nonclimatic differences can result in a polyclimax landscape where variations in soil, topography, or other microhabitat features can lead to a mosaic of climax types within the same climatic region. It should be reiterated that climate is the predominant force to affect the eventual outcome of succession on a regional level, it is, however, not the only one.

(2) Successional Trends

Ecologists have attempted to document successional processes in many different vegetation types over the past four to five decades. The first attempt to present broad generalizations about how various ecological characteristics change during the course of directional succession was made by Eugene Odum (1969). He presented 24 ecosystem characteristics that he hypothesized changed significantly during succession. Odum's work has since been scrutinized and amended so that some ecosystem characteristics have been added and some dropped. The successional trends of those ecosystem characteristics considered here are those that have generally been agreed upon to occur in most (but not all) systems.

Biomass and plant cover generally increase from early to late successional stages while physiognomy increases in complexity over the same time period. Early successional stages are typically characterized by "open" or "leaky" and less efficient nutrient cycles while later stages exhibit "tighter" or "closed" and more efficient nutrient cycles. Species diversity usually increases during the course of succession but is not always greatest at the climax[2]. Rather, diversity in many temperate forests is highest prior to the climax just before the tree canopy closes and eliminates some shade intolerant understory species. Early successional stages tend to be dominated by a greater proportion of r-selected species with K-selected species becoming more dominant as succession proceeds. Net primary production by the plant community may be entirely consumed at or near the climax resulting in no net addition of plant biomass. Thus at climax net ecosystem production (productivity of all trophic levels combined) is at or near zero and the system is simply maintaining itself from an energy perspective (Westman, 1985).

STABILITY OF ECOSYSTEMS

Ecosystem stability has several meanings depending on the perspective and context in which it has been used by various authors. The most straightforward definition and that utilized by Walter Westman (1978, 1985, 1986) and Michael Barbour *et al.* (1987) is simply the lack of change within an ecosystem or the pattern of fluctuations within an ecosystem over time. Other ecologists (e.g., MacArthur, 1955; May, 1973; Orians, 1975) have used the pace and manner of ecosystem recovery following disturbance (referred to as ecosystem resilience in this text) and/or the resistance of an ecosystem to change when disturbed (referred to as ecosystem inertia in this text) as definitions of stability. In order to distinguish the differences between ecosystem resilience and inertia (concepts which will be discussed later) this text will utilize the more common definition of stability promoted by Westman (1978, 1985, 1986) and Barbour *et al.* (1987).

(1) Diversity and Stability

While the different definitions of stability add to the general confusion surrounding this ecosystem characteristic it is important to initially consider the ecological and historical context of stability when it is treated as resilience and/or inertia. Over the past three decades ecosystem stability (i.e., resilience) was thought to increase as the complexity or diversity of a system increases. Thus the less diverse arctic ecosystems were thought to be fragile and the highly diverse tropical rainforests very resilient. The truth, of course, is just the opposite, those supposedly "fragile" arctic systems may be among the most resilient (Colinvaux, 1986) while experience has now shown that tropical rainforests, which once deforested recover very slowly, if at all, are among the least resilient. However, as S.J. McNaughton (1988:204) notes   ..."There is something almost mythological about the hypothesis that greater species diversity in ecological communities is associated with greater community stability. Like Hydra, cutting off one of its heads leads to two sprouting back." This controversial but seemingly straightforward notion has found its way into textbooks and into much of the ecological framework used to formulate management plans for many public lands (e.g., national parks, national forests, etc.) and in a variety of environmental impact assessments.

Robert MacArthur (1955) and D.R. Margalef (1957) used the Shannon-Wiener function H' and information theory to lay the theoretical foundation for diversity-stability hypothesis. H' which, as noted earlier, combines both richness and equitability as a measure of total diversity, was originally used to measure the probability of information transfer. In its original context the stability of the information network increased in proportion to the additional alternate channels of information flow provided. The mathematics of information theory when applied to food webs thus led to the enticing conclusion that the greater the number of alternate pathways for energy flow (i.e., the more species or complexity) the greater the stability of the system. However, as Paul Colinvaux (1986) points out, information linkages are designed to facilitate transfer of information whereas links in food webs are more likely to hinder the flow of energy due to natural selection maximizing the likelihood of avoiding predation. Robert May (1972, 1973) was one of the first to question the credibility of the stability-diversity hypothesis. Utilizing a similar mathematical elegance which had given credibility to the stability-complexity notion, May showed that food webs made of compartments or modules with strong interactions within them and weak interactions between tended to increase overall community stability. In sum, May demonstrated that species diversity does not necessarily lead to greater stability but that environmental stability (such as found in the tropics) can lead to greater species diversity.

The debate will likely be fueled by the recent publication of a field based study in midwestern grasslands (Tilman and Downing, 1994). The authors reported increased resistance (inertia) and resilience to drought induced changes in productivity in species rich plots relative to experimental plots with fewer species[3]. While this study may lend credence to the stability-diversity hypothesis, at least with respect to terrestrial grasslands, it should be noted that productivity is only one of many ecosystem properties that are likely to influence the overall integrity and homeostatic balance of an ecosystem. Indeed as Westman (1986:7) pointed out "...to relate the 'stability' of any ecosystem property to species diversity (or richness) is so reductionist as to be ultimately rather meaningless."

(2) Keystone Species

From an ecological perspective not all species are equal. The removal or reduction in abundance of some species may have little short or long-term effect on ecosystem stability. However, the removal of keystone species, those species that are critical to maintaining the stability and diversity of certain ecosystems, can have dramatic reverberations throughout the entire system. Robert Paine (1966, 1974, 1980) was one of the first ecologists to document the effects of removing a keystone species. He worked in the intertidal systems at Mukkaw Bay in Washington state. In some of these intertidal pools he removed all individuals of *Pisaster* (a starfish) the primary predator of the herbivorous invertebrates. Dramatic population shifts occurred in the systems where *Pisaster* was removed as the number of species decreased from 15 to 8 and the community became dominated by a mussel (*Mytilus californianus*). Other documented examples of keystone species include the role sea otters play in maintaining the integrity of kelp beds in Pacific nearshore communities (Estes and Palmisano, 1974) and the roles of black sage (*Salvia mellifera*) and purple sage (*Salvia leucophylla*) in controlling the abundance of understory herbs in the coastal shrublands of southern California (Westman, 1990).

ECOSYSTEM RESPONSE TO DISTURBANCE

The response of an ecosystem to disturbance[4] is largely dependent upon the disturbance type. Acute disturbances are intense biomass destroying activities that are relatively short-lived such as those inflicted by fires, floods, avalanches, hurricanes, tornados, or bulldozing. In contrast, chronic disturbances are less intense in nature but longer-lived such as air pollution, livestock grazing, trampling, soil erosion, or exposure to low-level radiation. Secondary succession (discussed earlier) is the process by which ecosystems recover following acute disturbance, however, there is no guarantee that the recovered state will closely resemble the predisturbed state.

(1) Retrogression

Ecosystems exposed to low-level but persistent disturbance (i.e., chronic) typically undergo retrogression, a process similar to but in the opposite direction of succession. Robert Whittaker and George Woodwell (1978) describe retrogression as the effects of chronic disturbance in reducing community structure and changing species composition in a way suggestive of succession in reverse. During the course of retrogression ecosystems become simplified as their characteristics are altered so as to resemble earlier successional stages. Such changes have been documented in systems exposed to grazing (Dyksterhuis, 1949), chronic gamma irradiation (Woodwell, 1967; 1970), and chronic air pollution (Winner and Bewley, 1978; Preston, 1988). It should be noted that while these affected communities are still functional systems, they have been both structurally and ecologically simplified to such a degree that ecosystem functions (e.g., nutrient cycling, soil binding, energy fixation, and gas absorption and release) may have been severely impaired.

(2) Ecosystem Inertia and Resilience

Inertia refers to the ability of a system to resist change when disturbed (Westman, 1978; 1985; 1986). Quantitatively inertia can be conceptualized as the degree of disturbance required to cause a significant change in some ecosystem property. For example, the intensity of grazing required to cause a shift in species composition or the air pollution dosages required to decrease the abundance of species X or Y. Some authors have simply referred to this ecosystem property as resistance (Barbour, *et al. 1987*; Harrison, 1979; Harwell *et al.*, 1977). In contrast, resilience is the pace, manner, and degree of ecosystem recovery after disturbance (Westman, 1978; 1985; 1986). As noted earlier the terms stability and resilience have been used interchangeably. However, to clarify the distinctions between these properties this text will define stability following Westman (1978, 1986) as the degree of ecosystem fluctuation in the absence of major exogenous disturbance. Resilience then refers to ecosystem recovery following acute or chronic exogenous disturbance.

Inertia is thus the resistance to change while resilience is in essence the pace, manner, and degree of recovery resulting from secondary succession after disturbance or change has occurred. Westman (1978, 1985, 1986) defined four major components of resilience: elasticity, amplitude, hysteresis, and malleability. In addition, Barry Fox and Marilyn Fox (1986) defined damping as a fifth component. The definitions of the five resilience components are given in Table II.3.

Table II.3 Components of Resilience

Component	Definition
ELASTICITY	The time required to restore the system to its initial pre-disturbance state.
AMPLITUDE	The zone of deformation (or disturbance) from which the system will still return to its initial pre-disturbance state.
MALLEABILITY	The degree to which the new steady state established after recovery differs from the original steady-state.

HYSTERESIS	The extent to which the path of degradation under chronic disturbance and of recovery when disturbance is removed are mirror images of each other.
DAMPING	The pattern of oscillations in an ecosystem property following disturbance.

Each of the above resilience components can be measured and quantified and thus provide great insight in the ability of natural ecosystems to recover from anthropogenic disturbances. Moreover, the degree, pace, and manner of recovery may also provide additional information about the ability of the recovered system to provide structures and functions in the same manner as the pre-disturbance state.

(3) Application of the Concepts of Inertia and Resilience

a. Inertia -- Measurement of inertia allows society to quantify the degree and magnitude of disturbance that results from economic activity which can occur before significant ecosystem change occurs. Westman (1985) suggested using the toxicological approach of an LD_{50}[5] or the degree of disturbance resulting in a 50% change in species composition or abundance (as measured by coefficients of community or percent similarity resemblance functions[6]) as measures of inertia. The selection of the 50% level is, of course, arbitrary and the specific level chosen would depend on the ecosystem monitored, the type of disturbance, and the ecosystem property measured. The latter is an important consideration because one ecosystem property may display a fairly high resistance to change while another may be very vulnerable to even low levels of disturbance. For example, species richness may not be affected even at moderate to high levels of disturbance; however, the relative abundance of individuals among those species may be drastically altered given the identical disturbance regime. In many situations ecosystem inertia may have to be assessed when experimental data are not available. Under these conditions mathematical and computer models that utilize information about the known physicochemical and ecological properties of a system may be used to estimate inertia. Unfortunately, while ecosystems vary in their degree of inertia (indeed some systems exhibit fairly high levels of resistance), it has become painfully clear that the degree of disturbance wrought by extractive and polluting economic activities has overwhelmed the inertia of many of the planet's ecosystems.

b. Elasticity -- The speed with which a disturbed system can recover to its pre-disturbed state is a resilience property that has been studied in some detail. Obviously, resource managers especially those involved in extracting renewable resources such as timber and fisheries would have a keen interest about the time required for a system to recover or "renew" itself. The key limitation here is the definition of the pre-disturbance state. Given the large amount of inherent variability in the natural world, the effects of stochastic events, and the vagaries of physical limiting factors one could hardly expect any recovered system to perfectly resemble the undisturbed state (i.e., a 100% similarity between the recovered and pre-disturbed states). Natural variation and sampling error may result in only a 70% to 95% similarity among replicate samples taken in the same undisturbed system (Westman, 1985). A more reasonable approach to the measurement of elasticity would be the time required for a disturbed state to return to a pre-disturbance similarity somewhat lower than 100%, perhaps a percent similarity of 50% to 75% depending on the magnitude of the pre-disturbance replicate similarity (Westman, 1985; 1986). As with inertia, the ecosystem property chosen for measurement is critical. One ecosystem property may return to within acceptable levels of the pre-disturbed state within a short time period while other properties may require much longer time frames.

c. Amplitude -- Numerous systems that have been severely disturbed in the past (e.g., tropical rainforests, some polluted rivers and streams) have not recovered to states even approximating the pre-disturbed system despite experiencing decades without any further disruption. Clearly, the initial disturbance, which was either too intense or persisted too long, changed the ecosystem to such a degree that recovery to the undisturbed state was no longer possible. This threshold disturbance beyond which recovery to the initial state can no longer occur is known as the amplitude. Knowledge of, for example, the amount of livestock packing on a grassland or degree of tree harvesting that can occur before the system is irreversible altered is of primary importance to resource and land managers. Specific populations within an ecosystem (e.g., particular plant, fish, or invertebrate species) are particularly prone to extirpation if harvesting techniques reduce their numbers below this threshold level. The "recovered" ecosystem may achieve a new and different steady-state relative to the pre-disturbed system but the level of structures and functions available in this new state is likely to be greatly reduced.

d. Malleability -- As noted above the new steady-state is not likely to be identical to the pre-disturbance state even if the approximation is within reasonable bounds. Alternatively, the new steady-state may radically differ from the initial state if the amplitude is exceeded. The degree by which the new steady-state differs from the initial is known as malleability. As with inertia and elasticity, percent similarity in species composition or abundance can be utilized to quantify the ecological distance between the two systems. However, the criteria used to ascertain when a new steady-state has been achieved must first be established. Westman (1978, 1985) suggested that a mean percent similarity change no larger than 5% from year to year over a several year period might be a reasonably good indicator of a stable state. The ecosystem property used to compute percent similarity is again of critical importance in ascertaining when an ecologically meaningful steady-state has indeed been established. Quantification of malleability may be a useful method for determining the extent to which the new steady-state provides ecosystem structures and functions relative to the undisturbed.

e. Hysteresis -- This resilience component can provide insight into the degree to which the path of degradation under chronic disturbance (retrogression) is useful in aiding in the recovery (secondary succession) of an ecosystem. For example, are the species that are the first to be extirpated the first to return during recovery (maximum hysteresis)? Usually those species that are the last to extirpate or decline significantly in abundance due to chronic disturbance are the first to return during recovery or secondary succession (hence little or no hysteresis). Typically K-selected species are the first to decline in the presence of chronic disturbance resulting in a simplified system usually dominated by more r-selected species. During secondary succession, however, r-selected species normally dominate in early seral stages while the K-selected species become more abundant during later successional stages. Thus knowledge of these processes could aid land and resource managers hasten the path of recovery by utilizing more ecologically sound rehabilitation practices.

f. Damping -- If a disturbance is acute (not chronic), such as fire or clearcutting of a forest, the degradation is more or less instantaneous and the measurement of hysteresis is not possible. Under such conditions the pattern of oscillations in an ecosystem property following disturbance or damping can be measured instead. The greater the degree of damping, the smaller the amplitudes of oscillation and the shorter their duration and hence the greater the elasticity or speed by which the system recovers. The effect of exogenous factors (such as subsequent disturbance) in decreasing damping and hence increasing the speed of recovery is obviously an important consideration when attempting to rehabilitate disturbed ecosystems.

While the above properties of inertia and resilience can increase understanding of ecosystem processes and how they are affected by anthropogenic, and usually economically motivated, disturbances, it should be clear that the ecosystem property (or properties) chosen for measurement can have a profound effect on the interpretation of the end results. Coefficients of community and percent similarity in species composition or abundance are the most common, but not the only, quantitative ecological indices utilized. Even these relatively simple indices vary greatly in their numerical value and ecological meaning depending on the ecosystem property used. If, for example, a qualitative approach is used and only species richness is noted a simple species list will suffice. The inherent assumption in this approach is, however, that all species are weighted equally regardless of their abundance[7]. Alternatively, if the investigator instead wishes to measure the species' relative abundances, a decision must be made as to which characteristic(s) will be used to quantify the relative abundance of each species. A variety of measures of relative abundance exist (e.g., density, productivity, foliar cover, basal area, frequency, or some combination of these) each with their own advantages and disadvantages depending on the plant or animal community in question. It is thus up to the investigator to chose the ecosystem property (or set of properties) that is most closely tied to the full suite of ecosystem structures and functions provided by the undisturbed system.

RELATING NATURE TO THE ECONOMY

Obviously, most, if not all, anthropogenic ecosystem disruptions are directly or indirectly motivated by economic behavior of some kind. Whether the activity is extractive in nature (e.g., timber harvesting, mining, fishing, or livestock grazing on natural grasslands) or the deposition of residuals (e.g., toxic wastes, municipal garbage, or air and water pollutants) into natural or semi-natural ecosystems, the short-term incentive is an economic gain to an individual or group of individuals (or sector of society). The long-term distributional consequences, however, may include greater economic costs often borne by individuals or segments of society other than those who benefited from the initial short-term gain. The economic consequences of anthropogenic induced ecosystem disruption and some preliminary considerations concerning the direct and indirect valuation of lost or impaired structures and functions will be considered below.

(1) Types of Ecosystem Structures

Recall that structures consist of the tangible features or products found within ecosystems. Some of these structures, such as timber, fossil fuels, minerals, or fisheries are commercially harvested or extracted for their economic value. Others do not have a direct harvestable value but may nonetheless be economically valuable in their more or less undisturbed state for recreational activities (e.g., camping, fishing, hunting, hiking, etc.). In addition, some structures have no apparent market value but may be important for asthetic, scientific, and ecological reasons. For example, it is difficult to assign an economic value on the peace and tranquilty of a pristine alpine meadow; or how often are soil bacteria, fungi, and invertebrates considered during the valuation of an ecosystem, yet they are critical for decomposition and nutrient cycling.

a. Renewable Resources -- Ecosystem structures are considered renewable if when harvested or otherwise utilized by humans they are capable of regenerating themselves. Usually only strictly biological entities such as trees or fisheries are considered renewable resources, however, other structures such as soil, which of course also contains living organisms, are capable of regeneration if not overutilized or allowed to erode. These resources must, however, be managed wisely with respect to their ecological constraints if they are to remain renewable.

b. Non-renewable Resources -- Some ecosystem structures, such as fossil fuels and mineral stocks, are considered non-renewable because they are present in finite quantities. Perhaps a more appropriate definition of a non-renewable resource is one which is used at a greater rate than it is replenished. Fossil fuels, for example, are continually being created in the earth's crust yet the rate at which humans extract them far exceeds their rate of replenishment. Under the latter definition even structures normally considered renewable could become non-renewable. A fishery when overfished and forced to extinction certainly can no longer replenish itself; or a clearcut forested area which subsequently experiences significant soil erosion and loss of nutrients may have difficulty regenerating.

(2) Economic Consequences of Ecosystem Disruption

When ecosystems are disrupted by human activities it is the economic consequences resulting from the loss of (or decrease in) structures that garners all or most of the attention. Moreover, it is usually the loss of marketable structures, whether they are harvested directly or accrue economic gain indirectly from recreational activities, that are even considered within the political and economic arena. As noted earlier many structures not valued by the market or considered economically important nonetheless play an important and often pivotal role in maintaining the integrity of natural ecosystems. One area that has received the least attention, and in some cases been ignored altogether, is the disruption of ecosystem functions. Recall ecosystem functions or nature's services are the dynamic processes of energy fixation, gas absorption and release, soil binding, decomposition, etc. that provide us with clean air and water and a homeostatic balance among living organisms and the physical environment. These services are not harvested, directly utilized, or even enjoyed by humans in the same fashion as ecosystem structures. Who would visit a national park or wilderness area to witness or watch decomposition or soil binding in a pristine natural environment? Despite the lack of explicit economic value, loss or disruption of ecosystem functions can impart a significant long-term economic toll on human societies. For example, overgrazing and poor land use management practices throughout the Great Plains in the latter part of the 19th and early part of the 20th centuries resulted in the Dust Bowl of the late 1920's and early 1930's. In this case, the lack of any consideration for the soil binding function led to massive dust storms and huge losses of topsoil and nutrients resulting in substantial economic costs and untold human misery. Even in today's relatively more enlightened climate, ecosystem functions such as absorption of pollutants by plants, the shading and cooling provided by vegetation canopies in urban heat islands, the water purification properties of intact wetlands, the fixation of nitrogen by microorganisms, or the role of ecosystems in maintaining the earth's radiation and gas balance remain undervalued or not valued at all during any discussion of resource management or decision making.

(3) Valuation of Ecosystems

Even though the above ecosystem attributes are typically ignored or undervalued some researchers have attempted to provide policy and decision makers with at least a first step in an attempt to more adequately quantify the value of the full array of ecosystem services and goods. Westman (1977, 1985) suggested the use of repair, replacement, and damage costs in any valuation of the costs accrued to societies from ecosystem disruption. In an attempt to evaluate the full monetary value of Louisiana wetlands Robert Costanza and Stephen Farber (cited in Holden, 1990) combined estimates of the commercial and recreational value of wetlands (i.e., economic value of structures) with the estimates of solar energy captured by plants (e.g., energy used to drive functions). Their estimates of GPP were converted into fossil fuel equivalents and subsequently into monetary units. The researchers concluded that if the state of Lousisana was concerned about its long-term future it would be charging $17,000 per acre for wetlands instead of the current market value, exclusive of mineral rights, of $300 to $500. While researchers are beginning to attempt to quantify the full array of ecosystem properties in terms of their real economic value, a number of major problems and obstacles exist (Dietz and van der Straaten, 1992; Alper, 1993).

a. Nature's Complexity -- The large degree of interconnectedness and accompanying complexity among the components of a natural ecosystem make it extremely difficult to measure and quantify with a great degree of precision the value of (or evaluate the effects of disturbance on) a single entity in isolation. Evaluating and quantifying the costs resulting from timber harvesting (which is federally subsidized on many public lands) can be illustrative of the problems that can arise. Some costs such as the building of logging roads and bridges and even the cost to replant trees may be easily measured. Estimation of other costs associated with soil erosion and subsequent nutrient loss, the sedimentation of streams and other aquatic systems, the filling of sediment catchment basins or sedimentation behind dams, or the changes in biodiversity that also result from timber harvesting are, however, more problematic.

The failure of compensatory mitigation of wetlands to meet the requirements of the "no net loss" policy underscores the problems encountered by the complexity of a natural system. The crux of this policy is based on the notion that no net loss of wetlands would be allowed to occur. However, a proposed development would be allowed to destroy an existing wetland as long as the developer agreed to mitigate the effect by reclaiming other wetlands or creating new ones. After ten years and thousands of mitigation projects the policy has done little to stem the tide of wetland loss. The problem is not that humans cannot create wetlands, but that they cannot create wetlands that provide the full array of functions found in the original natural systems.

Perhaps one of the greatest tributes to our lack of knowledge about the natural world is the fact that we have identified possibly fewer than 10% of the species living on the planet. Approximately 1.4 million of the earth's species have been cataloged. Wildlife biologists estimate that there may be as many as 10 to 100 million additional species yet to be discovered, many of which may go extinct before their existence to humans is known (Wilson, 1992).

b. Interactions Among Agents of Disturbance and Stressors -- A second obstacle with fully evaluting the effects of anthropogenic stressors and disturbance lies in the fact that each effect is typically analyzed and evaluated in isolation. When setting standards for potentially toxic chemicals, for example, the standards are derived by estimating the biological effect of each chemical separately. Living organisms (including humans) and ecosystems are not usually exposed to a single toxicant or stressor at any given time but are more often exposed to two or more potentially toxic agents simultaneously. While the cumulative effect of such simultaneous exposures is often additive (i.e., simply the sum of the effects in isolation) some toxicants or stressors can interact in a nonadditive fashion. The interaction may be an antagonistic one if the overall effects are less than additive or synergistic if greater than additive. It is the possible effects of synergisms that is of greatest concern since the potential for these interactions is rarely tested and their presence would result in a significant underestimation of the extent of toxicity or disturbance.

A number of ecological processes exacerbate the effects of certain pollutants or toxins. Some chemicals such as chlorinated hydrocarbons biomagnify and are concentrated as they move up the trophic ladder. The effect on organisms at higher trophic levels is thus much more pronounced than would be expected from the concentrations found in the physical environment. Moreover, some substances are transformed into more toxic agents by biotic and abiotic processes. DDT, for example, can be transformed into the more toxic DDE by microbes and nitrogen oxides and hydrocarbons are transformed via photochemical reactions into tropospheric O_3.

c. Short-Term vs. Long-Term Costs and Consequences -- A third major problem associated with the economic valuation of ecosystem disruption is inherent in the time frames within which the market operates and within which ecosystem processes occur. As noted earlier, small or even initially benign short-term effects can become manifested as major ecosystem disruptions in the long-term. Market processes, however, typically operate within much shorter time frames. It thus becomes difficult to estimate the true costs of some future long-term ecosystem pertubation within the context of short-term market forces.

d. Political Constraints -- The valuation of economically produced commodities and services so that they reflect the true environmental and societal costs they incur would, in most circumstances, be politically extremely unpopular. For example, H.M. Hubbard (cited in Alper, 1993) estimated that the cost of protecting the Persian Gulf shipping lanes adds an additional $23.50 per barrel of imported oil. He noted further that if all costs related to energy use (such as human illness, vegetation and crop damage, and corrosion) were internalized it would add between $100 to $300 billion to society's energy bill. Many of these costs are paid by society indirectly in the form of higher food prices, higher health insurance premiums, and taxes. If these costs were internalized and reflected in the price of a gallon of gasoline, for example, its price would more than quadruple (Alper, 1993). Such a valuation of the true environmental and health cost of energy is of course politically out of the question.

(4) Flows Between the Economy and Nature

The economy can be viewed as a process of material transformation where a series of exchanges or flows of matter link it to nature (Figure II.10). The producing side of the economy extracts renewable and nonrenewable resources

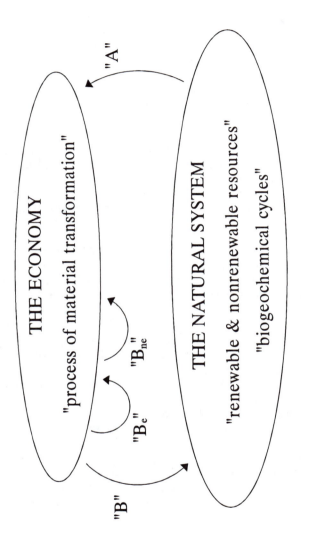

FIGURE II.10

from natural systems (flow "A") and transforms them into commodities (e.g., food, automobiles, books, clothes, etc.) and real capital (e.g., schools, factories, libraries, etc.). Flow "A" may also represent the use of intact ecosystem structures to produce capital as in the case of the economic activity generated by recreational uses of nature e.g., camping, fishing, hiking, hunting, etc.). Society consumes and uses the commodities and real capital and returns them to the natural system as residuals (flow "B"). These consumer and producer residuals are returned into a region's ecosystems in the form of solid waste, effluent discharges into waterbodies, or gaseous emissions into the atmosphere. Flow "Be" depicts a nation's ongoing economically viable recycling markets. In contrast, flow "Bne" is a depiction of a nation's attempt to recycle materials for which there are no existing economic markets. Within the disciplines of economics and law, flow "A" is the primary concern of natural resource economics and law while flow "B" is the primary concern of environmental economics and law.

The linkages in Figure II.10 underscore that the successful pursuit of economic growth (an ever larger and larger GDP) serves not only to enhance the real flows and dollar flows within the economy, but also serves to enhance both the flow of extracted resources into the economy (flow "A") and the deposition of residuals into the natural system (flow "B"). To some degree there are regional differences in the ability of natural processes to assimilate the residuals emanating from economic activities. These differences largely depend on a region's abiotic (primarily, but not exclusively, climate and soil) and biotic limiting factors. In many cases these residuals will be absorbed or assimilated with relatively few deleterious side effects. Similarly, some ecosystems will exhibit few disruptions from the extraction of the renewable and nonrenewable resources utilized by the economy. However, in other cases the ability of nature to assimilate economic residuals or recover from the mining or harvesting activities that accompany resource extraction may be exceeded (e.g., if the inertia and/or the amplitude of the system are exceeded). Under such circumstaces changes within the affected ecosystems may dramatically alter or destroy the full suite of structures and functions these systems provide (see previous sections for a fuller discussion of such changes) and inevitably incur some cost to society in the long-term.

ENDNOTES

1. Dominance diversity curves are graphical variations of heterogeneity indices that visually separate richness and equitability and thus do not suffer from the problems afflicting other such indices. These curves are constructed by plotting the species rank (most abundant to least abundant) along the abscissa and the corresponding importance values (as measured by the species' relative abundance) on a log scale along the ordinate. Species richness can be determined by the extent of the curve along the X axis while equitability is a function of the slope of the curve. A gentle slope indicates a large number of moderately abundant species with fewer dominant and rare species and hence a higher equitability. In contrast, communities with low equitability typically exhibit dominance diversity curves with greater slopes.

2. Some notable exceptions exist. In Californian shrublands (and other Mediterranean climate shrublands) diversity is highest in the early successional stages following a fire and decreases steadily as it approaches the climax.

3. The researchers compared a native prairie stand to three successional grasslands and found that the natural logarithm of pre-drought species richness and the natural logarithm of post-drought species richness had low but significant partial correlations of 0.21 and 0.184, respectively, with drought resistance.

4. A distinction between disturbance and stress will be made in this text. While disturbance refers to biomass destroying activities such as fire, grazing, cutting, etc., stress refers to biomass depressing activities such as the presence of suboptimal levels of nutrients, heat, moisture, or light.

5. An LD_{50} is the dosage of toxicant required to kill 50% of a population of organisms within a standardized time period such as 48 or 96 hours.

6. A number of coefficients of community (CC) exist for comparing communities utilizing presence and absence data. Two commonly utilized CC's include Jaccard's and Czekanowski's indices which take the following form:

$$\text{Jaccard's CC} = (c/(a + b - c)) \times 100$$
$$\text{Czekanowski's CC} = (2c/(a + b)) \times 100$$

Where a is the total number of species in site A, b the total number of species in site B, and c the number of species in common between the two sites.

In contrast to CC's, percent similarity functions use quantitative data on the relative abundance of each species; one of the most common forms is:

$$\text{Percent Similarity} = \frac{200\Sigma(\text{minimum a, b})}{\Sigma(a + b)}$$

Where minimum a, b is the lesser abundance of a given species present in both sites, a is the abundance of all species in site A, and b is the abundance of all species in site B.

7.   If species richness is used as an ecosystem attribute or coefficients of community are used for comparison purposes, each species is inherently weighted equally because they will be noted as present whether only one individual or a thousand individuals inhabit a particular community.

REFERENCES

Aldous, P. 1993. Tropical Deforestation: Not Just a Problem in Amazonia. *Science* 259 (5 March): 1390.

Alper, J. 1993. Protecting the Environment With the Power of the Market. *Science* 260 (25 June): 1884-1885.

Barbour, M.G., Burk, J.H., and Pitts, W.D. 1987. *Terrestrial Plant Ecology*, 2nd edition. Menlo Park: Benjamin/Cummings.

Clements, F.E. 1916. Plant Succession, an Analysis of the Development of Vegetation. *Carnegie Institution of Washington Publication* 242: 1-512.

Colinvaux, P. 1986. *Ecology*. New York: John Wiley and Sons.

Dietz, F.J. and van der Straaten, J. 1992. Rethinking Environmental Economics: Missing Links between Economic Theory and Environmental Policy. *Journal of Economic Issues* 26 (March): 27-51.

Dyksterhuis, E.J. 1949. Condition and Management of Range Land Based on Quantitative Ecology. *Journal of Range Management* 2: 104-115.

Estes, J.A. and Palmisano, 1974. Sea Otters: Their Role in Structuring Nearshore Communities. *Science* 185: 1058-1060.

Fox, B.J. and Fox, M.D. 1986. Resilience of Animal and Plant Communities to Human Disturbance. In *Resilience in Mediterranean-Type Ecosystems*, ed. B. Dell, A.J.M. Hopkins, and B.B. Lamont, 39-64. Dordrecht: Dr. W. Junk Publishers.

Gleason, H.A. 1926. The Individualistic Concept of Plant Association. *Bulletin of the Torrey Botanical Club* 53: 7-26.

Harrison, G.W. 1979. Stability Under Environmental Stress: Resistance, Resilience, Persistence and Variability. *American Naturalist* 113: 659-669.

Harwell, M.A., Cropper, W.P., and Ragsdale, H.L. 1977. Nutrient Recycling and Stability: A Reevaluation. *Ecology* 58: 660-666.

Holden, C. 1990. Multidisciplinary Look at a Finite World. *Science* 249 (6 July): 18-19.

Kerr, R.A. 1990. New Greenhouse Report Puts Down Dissenters. *Science* 249 (3 August): 481-482.

Kormondy, E.J. 1976. *Concepts in Ecology*, 2nd edition. Englewood Cliffs: Prentice-Hall.

MacArthur, R.H. 1955. Fluctuations of Animal Populations, and a Measure of Community Stability. *Ecology* 36: 533-536.

MacArthur, R.H. and Wilson, E.O. 1967. *The Theory of Island Biogeography*. Princeton: Princeton University Press.

Margalef, D.R. 1957. La Teoria de la Información en Ecologia. *Memo. del la Real Acad. De Cienc. y Artes de Barcel.* 23: 79.

May, R.M. 1972. Will a Large Complex System be Stable? *Nature* 238: 413-414.

May. R.M. 1973. *Stability and Complexity in Model Ecosystems*. Princeton: Princeton University Press.

McNaughton, S.J. 1988. Diversity and Stability. *Nature* 333 (19 May): 204-205.

Odum, E.P. 1969. The Strategy of Ecosystem Development. *Science* 164: 262-270.

Paine, R.T. 1966. Food Web Complexity and Species Diversity. *American Naturalist* 100: 65-75.

Paine, R.T. 1974. Intertidal Community Structure: Experimental Studies on the Relationship Between a Dominant Competitor and its Principle Competitor. *Oecologia* 15: 93-120.

Paine, R.T. 1977. Controlled Manipulations in the Marine Intertidal Zone and Their Contributions to Ecological Theory. *Acad. Nat. Sci. Phila. Spec. Pub.* 12: 245-270.

Orians, G.H. Diversity, Stability and Maturity in Natural Ecosystems. In *Unifying Concepts in Ecology*, ed. W.H. van Dobben and R.H. Lowe-McConnel, 64-65. The Hague: Junk.

Preston, K.P. 1988. Effects of Sulphur Dioxide Pollution on a Californian Coastal Sage Scrub Community. *Environmental Pollution* 51: 179-195.

Rosenberg, N.J. 1974. *Microclimate: The Biological Environment*, New York: John Wiley and Sons.

Ramensky, L.G. 1924. The Basic Lawfulness in the Structure of Vegetation Cover (in Russian). *Vestnik opytnogo dela Sredne-Chernoz. Obl.*, 37-73. Voronezh.

Ricklefs, R.E. 1990. *Ecology*, 3d edition. New York: W.H. Freeman.

Simpson, E.H. 1949. Measurement of Diversity. *Nature* 163: 688.

Swartz, R.C. 1980. Application of Diversity Indices in Marine Pollution Investigations. In: *Biological Evaluation of Environmental Impacts*, Report FWS/OBS-80/26 U.S. Dept. of Interior, Fish and Wildlife Service and Council on Environmental Quality, Washington, D.C.: 230-237.

Tilman, D. and Downing, J.A. 1994. Biodiversity and Stability in Grasslands. *Nature* 367 (27 January): 363-365.

Westman, W.E. 1977. How Much are Nature's Services Worth? *Science* 197: 960-964.

Westman, W.E. 1978. Measuring the Inertia and Resilience of Ecosystems. *Bioscience* 28 (November): 705-710.

Westman, W.E. 1985. *Ecology, Impact Assessment, and Environmental Planning*. New York: John Wiley and Sons.

Westman, W.E. 1986. Resilience: Concepts and Measures. In *Resilience in Mediterranean-Type Ecosystems*, ed. B.Dell, A.J.M. Hopkins, and B.B. Lamont, 5-19. Dordrecht: Dr. W. Junk Publishers.

Westman, W.E. 1990. Managing for Biodiversity: Unresolved Science and Policy Questions. *Bioscience* 40 (January): 26-33.

Whittaker, R.H. 1975. *Communities and Ecosystems*. New York: Macmillan.

Whittaker, R.H. and Woodwell, G.M. 1978. Retrogression and Coenocline Distance. In *Ordination of Plant Communities* 2nd edition, ed. R.H. Whittaker, 51-70. The Hague: Junk.

Wilhm, J.K. and Dorris, T.C. 1968. Biological Parameters for Water Quality Criteria. *Bioscience* 18: 477-481.

Wilson, E.O. 1992. *The Diversity of Life*. New York: W.W. Norton.

Winner, W.E. and Bewley, J.D. 1978. Contrasts Between Bryophytes and Vascular Plant Synecological Responses in an SO_2-stressed White Spruce Association in Central Alberta. *Oecologia* 33: 311-325.

Woodwell, G.M. 1967. Radiation and the Patterns of Nature. *Science* 156: 461-470.

Woodwell, G.M. 1970. Effects of Pollution on the Structure and Physiology of Ecosystems. *Science* 168: 429-433.

CHAPTER III

THE STATE

COOPERATION AND CONFLICT

However admirable it may seem to argue for maintaining the quality of the environment or display concern over the dissipation of a nation's natural resources, few areas of public policy have produced conflicts of such a heightened magnitude both within nations as well as between nations. It is to the channeling of these environmental conflicts and into the realm of public policy to which we now turn.

With regard to natural resource and environmental matters, a society is perceived as both a cooperative venture for mutual advantage where and when there are an identity of interests and, as well, an arena of conflict where there exists a mutual interdependence of conflicting claims or interests. The manner in which a society structures its political/legal institutions -- (1) to enhance the scope of its cooperative natural resource and environmental endeavors, (2) to channel internal natural resource and environmental conflicts toward resolution, and (3) to institutionalize mechanisms for accomplishing legal change, -- helps shape the character of life in that society. Within this conceptual model, individuals are assumed to take actions individually and collectively, in both the private and public sectors. It is posited that individual actions are taken to advance their individual interests or their individual perceptions of the public interest.

In contemplating the structure of its governing institutions, a nation must be concerned with both (a) those institutional structures that will help promote cooperation among parties of interest to natural resource and environmental issues, as well as (b) those institutional structures that help channel natural

resource and environmental conflicts. At the most general level, a society is
confronted with questions as to what will be the nature of its underlying
constitution and what will be the *initial* structure of the institutions that will go
towards shaping the character of life in that society -- both with respect to the
nation's economy as well as its environment.   Whether one or another
political/legal institution is seen to emerge in a society in response to the natural
resource and environmental issues confronting it, the emergence and legitimacy
of these institutions can be interpreted, in part, as a response (at the most
fundamental level) of the citizens comprising that society .

STAGES OF CHOICE[1]

   The selection or establishment of a specific set of institutions, and thus the
character of life in a society, is the product of choice. What the field of law and
economics has to say about some of these matters is pertinent to a wide array of
issues beyond the environment. While this chapter is intended to be quite general
and have relevance beyond natural resource and environmental issues, as and
where appropriate, this chapter will incorporate natural resource and
environmental examples to help clarify the general points being made.
   With respect to law and economics, much of the literature has focused
attention on three different stages of choice. First, it becomes necessary to
describe and understand the emergence of the most basic social contract that binds
its people together. This can be termed the *constitutional stage of choice*.
Second, it is necessary to describe and understand both the structuring and the
revising or restructuring of the political/legal institutional decision-making
processes -- the so-called *institutional stage of choice*. Finally, the consequent
economic impacts of the prevailing or potentially revised legal relations governing
society must be analyzed and understood -- the *economic impact stage of choice*.
In attempting to address these concerns, most of those contributing to the
literature of law and economics have divided their labors to describe these three
different levels of choice (see Figure III.1).

   (1) Constitutional Stage of Choice

   In order to understand the nature of the choices necessary at the
constitutional stage, it is useful to start society off in a conceptual state of
anarchy. Individuals will then contemplate the opportunity costs associated with
the protective-defensive resource diversions that are necessary and essential for
life under a system of anarchy. Once they recognize the potential prospects for
improvement in the character of their economic life brought on by establishing
a social contract or constitution, they will enter into some form of social contract

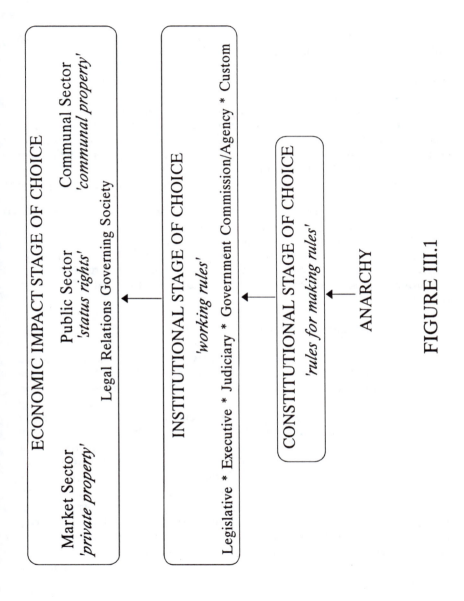

FIGURE III.1

or formally adopt a constitution. In establishing the constitution, the individuals will seek to spell out the behavioral limits of what is and what is not mutually acceptable conduct and lay out the so-called *rules for making rules*. It must be noted that while the established constitution is typically thought to have only a subtle effect on the allocation and distribution of resources, particularly with respect to natural resource and environmental policy, that subtle impact cannot go ignored. In addition, since constitutions are not immutable, the methods by which constitutional rules can be revised are developed at this level of choice. Further, it should be noted that the relationships among emergent institutions are also partially resolved at the constitutional stage of choice.

The essential point to be understood here is that whatever institutions come to characterize a society, they owe their development, existence, and legitimacy to the initial choices made at the constitutional stage of choice. Once the constitution is framed, it will then provide the basis for the emergence of a broad assemblage of legal-economic institutions -- institutions that will more directly affect the allocation of resources in society as well as act to safeguard the integrity of the many ecosystems that make up a nation's environment. The structuring of these legal-economic institutions constitutes the institutional stage of choice.

(2) The Institutional Stage of Choice

The institutional stage of choice focuses directly on the structure of the political/legal institutions (more commonly referred to as *the State*) as well as the revision of those institutional structures. It is the specific *working rules* -- the complex of set of rules that give rise to the institutional decision-making processes -- that are at center stage. More often than not the decision-making processes of an institution are formally worked out by the institution itself in developing its own working rules. In addition, the decision-making processes of a legal institution are partially established by the rules worked out at the constitutional stage of choice; and as well, they are also a partial function of the decisions of other institutions worked out often under complex procedures. An example of this would be a court decision which imposes certain restrictions or obligations either upon the decision-making processes of a legislative body regarding environmental statutes or the decision-making processes of a government agency regarding the regulation of natural resources.

As in the case of constitutions, legal institutions are not set in stone, but rather are themselves a response to economic needs and, as such, can and do undergo structural revisions. A full understanding of the role of working rules is fundamental in resolving disputes regarding natural resource use or environmental quality. Sophisticated industrialists (as well as many environmental lawyer/lobbyists) are fully aware of the leverage obtained in the initial structuring or the revising of working rules. Those who do not understand the crucial role of working rules are often found in emotional street demonstrations.

From a policy standpoint, the primary difficulty in promulgating working rules lies in trying to design legal-economic institutions so as to provide the decision makers the proper incentive structures to correctly channel behavior so as to help enable a society to internalize environmental externalites and to guide decision makers in the extraction of natural resources. In the simplest of terms, "all bureaucracies are not created equal." With respect to the fashioning or the redesigning of working rules, much work remains to be done to identify which institutional structures go towards enhancing the efficiency of legal institutions in accomplishing their stated environmental and natural resource goals. The extent to which the institutions can be so structured, they will directly affect a nation's natural resources and the integrity of its environment.

Changes in the working rules of legal institutions will revise the decision-making processes of those institutions and, as a result, may alter the institutional choices that directly impact the legal relations governing a society -- the extant structure of property rights. It is these choices as to the structure of property rights to which we now turn by exploring the economic impact stage of choice inasmuch as (a) it is this stage of choice that comprises the most prominent interface between law and economics, and (b) it has the most direct relationship to natural resource and environmental economic policy.

(3) The Economic Impact Stage of Choice

Conceptually, it is useful to begin with the notion of three distinct property right systems for organizing and controlling the allocation of society's scarce resources: the market sector, the public sector, and the communal sector. Initially each sector is treated as if it exists separate and apart from the other sectors. As will be seen, typically, all three systems operate contemporaneously to allocate resources.

a. The Market Sector -- In the pure market sector, all property rights are held privately as bundles of fee simple absolute rights. According to the conventional legal-economic definition of property rights, what are owned by individuals are not goods or resources but are the rights to use goods and resources. Armen A. Alchian and Harold Demsetz (1973:17) stated, "What are owned are socially recognized rights of action." Thus, as outlined by Alan Randall (1981:148), in the pure market sector, property rights must have four characteristics. They must be:

- Completely specified, so that it can serve as a perfect system of information about the rights that accompany ownership, the restrictions upon those rights, and the penalties for their violation.

- Exclusive, so that all rewards and penalties resulting from an action accrue directly to the individual empowered to take action (i.e., the owner).

- Transferable, so that rights may gravitate to their highest-value use.

- Enforceable and completely enforced. An unenforced right is no right at all.

With this structure of private property rights established by the individuals in a society, acting through their institutions and with the market as the system of social control, it is then possible for the individuals to further enhance their welfare by specializing and engaging in exchange through trade. This process of trade is conventionally viewed as a purely voluntary endeavor and, as characterized here, it is what transpires in the market sector. The voluntary nature of this market process is such that no individual will engage in a trade that leaves him worse off. The final allocative outcome will be arrived at once all the gains from trade have been exhausted in both exchange and production. Thus, given a set of private property rights so structured and given some initial distribution of rights, barring externalities and the problem of public goods, one can expect, consistent with the duality theorem, the market outcome to provide a Pareto efficient allocation of resources (in terms of Table I.1, MBs = MCs).

b. Public Sector -- The public sector is yet another arena for organizing and controlling the allocation of resources in a society. In this idealized sector the allocation and distribution of all resources will be determined by the State. That is, in response to the individuals who comprise the society, the legal-economic institutions will define and assign *status rights* which are, in effect, eligibility requirements for individuals to gain access to goods and resources.[2] Status rights are rights to goods and resources which are exclusive, nontransferable, and are provided to individuals at the discretion of either the local, the state, or the federal level of government. Thus, the provision of status rights may be conceived of as "government regulation" in its broadest sense. As such, political-legal institutions are understood to make a broad spectrum of decisions that give rise to status rights.

With the public sector as the system of social control, the emergent structure of status rights has a direct impact on the allocation of society's scarce natural resources and environmental policy. However, unlike the market sector resource allocations, within the public sector there are no spontaneous mechanisms for ensuring that decision makers in the public sector will make public policy pronouncements that are economically efficient. This problem is partially offset by the extent to which public sector decisions are based on benefit cost calculations -- in such cases, public sector decisions can be said to approach a Kaldor-Hicks efficient allocation of resources.[3]

c. Communal Sector -- Finally, individuals in a society, acting through their legal-economic institutions, may decide that commodities or resources will be communally owned and hence equally available to all (i.e., non-exclusive) and thus, nontransferable. In this case, rights would be assigned equally to each individual, resulting in a communal allocation of the common property resource which would only be allocatively efficient if supply exceeds demand at a zero price. If supply does not exceed demand at a zero price and society nonetheless retains the resource under communal ownership, the resource will be overused.[4]

d. The Complex Legal-Economic Arena -- Typically, western societies are structured so that the character of life is determined by all three systems of social control: the market sector, the public sector, and the communal sector. The relative scope and content of each of the systems of social control is the result of a collective determination of those who prevailed in choice-making processes in the political/legal economic arena.

Figure III.1 is intended to integrate the three stages of choice -- the constitutional, institutional, and economic impact stage together with the market, public and communal sector. The participants in the political/legal economic arena will (from the bottom up) establish a constitution so as to avoid the pitfalls and inefficiencies of anarchy; they will set in place working rules in structuring their legal-economic institutions; and they will structure the legal relations governing society -- private property rights, status rights, and communal rights, -- giving rise to the private, public and communal sectors, respectively.

Members of society, in attempting to promote economic growth and development as well as fostering actions to enhance and protect their environment and natural resources, will act both individually and collectively to revise the constitution, to structure and restructure the institutional working rules, and to alter the property rights (be they private, status, or communal) in the market, public, and communal sectors in order to achieve an allocation of resources that will enhance their individual welfare. This is accomplished under the recognition that neither (1) the constitution, (2) the decision-making processes of the legal institutions (i.e., the working rules), nor (3) the legal relations governing the size and scope of the market, public, and communal sectors are given immutably by

nature but are themselves a response to economic needs and flexible in response
to changes in those needs.

In summary, altering the *law* (i.e., changing the legal relations governing
society in any one or all of the three sectors) has a direct impact upon economic
performance including environmental quality. The underlying logic suggests the
following line of reasoning:

Δ law / working rules --> Δ incentive structure --> Δ institutional behavior -->
Δ economic performance --> Δ natural resources & environmental quality

It should be noted that the particular construction set forth in this section
parallels that which Walter Ullmann (1966) has described as "the ascending theme
of government and law." He traces the origins of this conception to the late 13th
century.   It is a conception of government and law where the individual is
perceived as sovereign -- not as a mere subject but as a citizen -- and where the
government and law owe their legitimacy to the *consent* of the sovereign
individuals. With greater robustness, Thomas Hobbes and John Locke, later in
the 17th century, developed a parallel conception of government and law wherein
the principal function of the government was seen to be, among other things, to
protect the purported "well-settled" sovereign natural rights held by individuals.

While the characterization of law and economics described in this section,
more or less follows the general contours of the ascending theme of government
and law, it is not the only theme that can describe the origin and thus legitimacy
of the prevailing constitution and government institutions.   Ullmann also
presented what he termed the "descending theme of government and law." His
characterization purports to describe much of pre-late 13th century Europe. As
elaborated upon by James S. Coleman (1974:72-76), this conception is not unlike
the ideas of rights and sovereignty latter developed by Jean-Jacques Rousseau and
Karl Marx.   The descending theme of government and law suggests that
sovereignty is located in the state with government there as the collective
instrument to implement the will of society. If founded in this manner, then the
constitution and government institutions gain their recognition and legitimacy
accordingly. It should be noted that while the argument set forth in this chapter
implies some form of democratic government, perhaps more consistent with
Ullman's "ascending theme," the essential point -- that the legal-economic
institutions have a direct impact on the allocation and distribution of resources --
is equally valid with respect to choices made by institutions of non-democratic,
coercive governments -- and in either case, both natural resources and the
environment are impacted.

(4) Examples of Natural Resource and Environmental Choice

It is important to understand the nature of the choices made at the constitutional, institutional, and economic impact stages of choice. Some specific examples may help to further understand what is at issue here. First, at a general level, at the constitutional stage of choice the basic elements of the social contract between individuals and their environment and natural resources will be set in place; the fundamental "rules for making rules" will be established and thereafter may undergo revision. For instance, within a nation's constitution there is the issue of whether environmental protection is considered a fundamental right retained by the individual, thereby enjoying the protected status as are other fundamental rights, or whether the constitutional provision is a mere goal or general statement of public policy.[5] In addition, the choices that govern which institutions will finally prevail over others in making choices (for example, to provide a system of checks and balances in the court's review of natural resource and environmental regulations or procedures) must be decided.

Further, working through the institutions, at the institutional stage of choice, individuals restructure institutions by altering working rules. Examples of what are involved at the institutional stage of choice include individuals attempting to *establish* or *alter* the following: (1) legislature - the rules for determining legislative committee structures so as to make clear what committees oversee the nation's renewable and nonrenewable natural resources and the rules for serving on those committees; (2) judiciary - the criteria as to who may/may not have standing in a court of law regarding environmental disputes; the rules that determine the role of intervenors at environmental hearings; and the rules of evidence in environmental cases; (3) government agencies - the method or procedure by which environmental standards or criteria are arrived at by such institutions as the E.P.A. or the F.D.A.,...etc.; (4) the criteria and/or the processes for obtaining pollution permits or obtaining the rights to as well as the rates of extraction of natural resources; and (5) the scope of natural resource or environmental actions that come under the notion of executive privilege.

Finally, at the economic impact stage of choice, individuals may work to revise property rights, and in doing so, they ultimately alter the legal relations among members of society and thereby redetermine (perhaps only incrementally) the relative scopes of the market, public and communal sectors in the society. It is important to understand that the nature of the choices made at the economic impact stage of choice are quite different than the choices made at the institutional stage of choice. Here individuals do not alter the working rules but work to alter property rights and thereby directly influence the decisions in the private, public and communal sectors.

For example, (1) they may work to determine which resources will be directly under the state's supervision via status rights (e.g., more or less wilderness area; more or less wetlands) or alternatively, held as private property with use dictated by the individual owner in the market sector. (2) They may attempt to set status rights in place through a host of public sector actions, for example in taking positions at legislative hearings in the drafting of environmental statutes, or channeling input into government agency or commission pronouncements on natural resource or environmental policies, or by defining specific eligibility requirements for individuals to gain access to certain services (egs., testing and screening for potential risks to health care), or through judge and jury verdicts in both natural resource and environmental litigation. (3) They may work to enhance or diminish the scope of residential, commercial, and industrial zoning restrictions. (4) They may attempt to have specific environmental criteria or standards adopted for the "green labeling" of consumer products. (5) They may lobby to have a parcel of land made readily available for private development or have the same parcel declared communal property for conservation or wilderness purposes. (6) They may attempt to affect the assignment of rights in such issues as to assign the right to an upstream chemical firm to allow it to dump its residuals into the stream or instead have the right assigned to the downstream farmer who uses the water for crop irrigation to have unpolluted water available. And finally, (7) individuals may argue to have environmental commissions either closely monitor and strictly enforce standing environmental laws or rarely monitor and thus loosely enforce the same laws.

All of the above examples are intended only to illustrate that individual participants in the political/legal economic arena can restructure (1) their constitution, (2) their institutions and (3) work to revise property right structures through the prevailing institutions and thereby reshape the ultimate character of economic life and the natural environment within which they live.

THE INTEGRATION OF THE NATURAL SYSTEM, THE ECONOMY, AND THE STATE

(1) The Role of the State

From the vantage point of the already established relationships between the *natural system* and the *economy*, we are now in a position to incorporate the *state* into this conceptual model (see Figure III.2). Recall from Chapter II, flow "A" represented the extraction of renewable and nonrenewable resources from a nation's natural resource endowment, while flow "B" represented the residuals returning to the nation's ecosystems having gone through the economy's process of material transformation. As depicted in Figure III.2, the state is perceived as

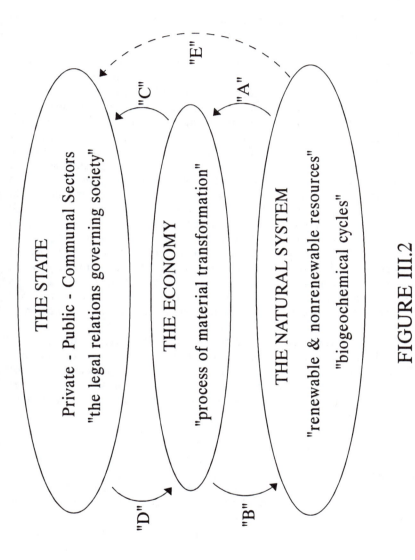

FIGURE III.2

the primary vehicle for making and implementing public policy. It is important to recognize that in most western societies, the state's primary linkages are to its economy.

Flow "C" attempts to depict that which emerges from the economy to the state. The primary flow here is that of *information*. It is that enormous array of government data (including both microeconomic and macroeconomic data) that is required to set in place executive, legislative, and administrative policy regarding the entire economy -- the information necessary for formulating (a) monetary and fiscal policy, (b) agricultural policy, (c) transportation and energy policy, (d) urban programs, (e) industrial policies...etc. *plus* (f) natural resource and (g) environmental policy. The economic information is typically that which reflects the present state of the various sectors of the entire economy (information in the form of "feedback"). One can juxtapose this information to the theoretical role of the information provided by an environmental impact statement, depicted by flow "E". "E" -- an environmental impact statement -- can be interpreted as an attempt to "feed forward" to the political/legal institutions the potential irreversible and irretrievable commitments of resources and the environmental impacts *before* a major project is undertaken. It should be clear that any nation that chooses not to have this environmental information feed *forward* to its choice-making institutions will continually be facing (in an ad hoc manner) yet another "natural resource or environmental crisis" so long as information is provided after the fact.

Flow "D" depicts *government policy decisions*, decisions that in most western societies often have as a high priority the encouragement of economic growth and development of the aggregate economy. If successful, the government's economic growth and development policies will serve to foster per capita growth in the GDP and thereby increase the number of jobs and enhance the nation's income and wealth. Flow "D" represents the whole plethora of decisions that emanate from government, including monetary and fiscal policies, specific policies regulating public utilities, energy, transportation, and industry and agriculture,...etc. In addition, as mentioned above, it is within flow "D" that natural resource and environmental policies are promulgated along with the full array of other, often competing policies, to meet a nation's many goals.

Thus, from the vantage point of the conceptual model presented here, the maintenance of the ecological integrity of the natural system is a direct function of (1) the natural resource extractions from the natural system "A" and (2) the residuals deposited back into the environment "B" as directly related to economic activity. Based on the data and information acquired by the state, "C", public policies "D" that increase the economic activity (GDP) will enhance the flow rates in the economy. However, the important point to be emphasized here is that, if the government policies are successful, the enhanced economic growth together with the higher per capita income -- because of the economy's linkages to the many ecosystems comprising the natural system -- will enhance both the rates of extraction from the natural system and the rates of depositing residuals back into the environment.

It is interesting to note that many classical economists thought that the economy was more apt to encounter limits on the depletion side (a so to speak "running out of nonrenewable resources") while in fact, the main limits seem to be occurring on the pollution side. One possible explanation of this phenomena is that most often, with the private ownership of many renewable and nonrenewable resources, the costs are private and thereby provide information for the stewardship of those natural resources. Alternatively, historically up to the 1960s, with the waste absorption capacity of the environment held under common property ownership, the costs associated with the residuals were external resulting in the persistent overloading of ecosystems (Stokes, 1992:128).

Of course, to some extent, both the rates of extraction and the rates of depositing residuals, "A' and "B" respectively, can be offset by new technologies and population control programs. But this model does not assume a quick technological fix for all of a nation's extractions from and residuals back into the environment. These cumulative impacts, once beyond the regionally specific assimilative capacity of a nation's ecosystems, will begin to undermine the ecological integrity of the impacted regional environments. Unless the state promulgates and fully enforces meaningful natural resource and environmental policies that take full account of these impacts on its ecosystems -- impacts due to both the extractions *and* the residuals -- it will continue to channel economic growth and development in such a way so as to destroy the ecological integrity of the environment. What the model attempts to draw attention to is the fact that societies must make choices in finding remedies. These choices can be made at the constitutional stage of choice, and/or by fashioning working rules at the institutional stage of choice, and/or at the economic impact stage of choice where private property rights, status rights, and communal property can be structured to protect a nation's environment.

As we proceed through a review of the legal-economic aspects of several environmental and natural resource policies, it is necessary to keep in mind the three property right structures described in this chapter -- the private property rights, the status rights, and communal property -- and the consequent incentives created. One of the most fundamental points to be made in Chapters IV and V which outline the spectrum of remedies to natural resource and environmental problems, is that each remedy involves either (a) including or altering certain constitutional provisions, (b) specifying certain working rules, and/or (c) placing the rights to the natural resources or the residual-receiving environmental media (the air, land resources, or water), directly or implicitly, into one of the three rights structures.

Recall, the private market sector is the arena in which private property rights are defined and assigned (hence exclusive), enforced, and subsequently transferred among the parties so as to exhaust gains from trade. The public sector is made up of the whole array of status rights across the full range of government institutions. In the public sector, resources are allocated under the stated government regulations -- status rights. And finally, the communal sector is that sector where rights to resources are set up as communal property, nonexclusive and nontransferable. The chosen legal relations governing that society -- the mix of private property, status rights, and communal rights -- will directly affect the economic performance of the mixed market economy, that is, the economic performance in its private, its public, and its communal sectors and ultimately the quality and ecological integrity of the nation's environment.

More specifically, the state, in formulating environmental policy, must choose to place the rights to the environmental media at issue - for example, an air shed, or lake basin, or river valley ecosystem...etc. into either (a) the private market sector to be held as private property; (b) the public sector under state supervision (under either a federal, state, or local government entity) through the specification of status rights; or (c) place the resource in the communal sector for all to use to the exclusion of no one.

In a like manner, the extraction of renewable and non-renewable resources from the ecosystem will be impacted by the government's decision as to whether to place the rights to these resources into the private market sector; the public sector under state supervision with use dictated by specified status rights; or the communal sector under communal rights. That is, if there is a change in the law -- for example, (a) a change in the definition or assignment of a private property right, or (b) a change in a working rule that alters the manner by which a judicial, legislative or bureaucratic environmental decision is to be reached, or (c) the altering of the eligibility requirement underlying a status right that enables a firm to extract a natural resource from state-owned land, or (d) expanding or diminishing the scope of communal rights to beachfront property -- such changes will alter incentives within the market and/or public and/or communal sectors, which in turn alters the behavior of individuals operating within those sectors, all of which impacts upon the economic performance of the mixed-market economy. And, as we have seen so clearly in Figure III.2, economic performance has a direct impact upon the ecological integrity of a nation's ecosystems and thus the quality of the environment.

In short:

$$\text{\tiny ▵} \text{ Law } ---> \quad \text{\tiny ▵} \text{ Economic Performance } ---> \begin{cases} \text{\tiny ▵} \text{ Environment Quality} \\ \\ \text{\tiny ▵} \text{ Conservation of Natural Resources} \end{cases}$$

In this context an understanding of the role of incentives is crucial -- particularly with regard to ex ante *versus* ex post analysis. When it comes to fashioning working rules, property rights, and status rights in an attempt to enhance environmental quality or regulate the extraction of natural resources, it is important to keep in mind the differing long-term versus the short-term effects of adopting one structure of working rules and/or rights over other possible structures. This is especially significant when courts are litigating disputes and a judge is being relied on to decide environmental and natural resource cases. As Judge Frank Easterbrook has pointed out, one must be careful to distinguish between "ex post" versus "ex ante" analysis in deciding cases. He stresses that courts are often in a position of deciding whether (by exercising what he terms ex post thinking, with an emphasis on doing what is "fair") to confer short-term benefits on certain parties of interest in a case due to the very difficult (and perhaps sympathetic) position these parties may find themselves, while perhaps at the same time creating incentives (that should have been anticipated but are not except in ex ante analysis) that enhance the number of individuals in theses difficult positions resulting in significant additional long-run societal costs. He stated:

> The first line of inquiry...is whether the Justices take an ex ante or an ex post perspective in analyzing issues. Which they take will depend, in part, on the extent to which they appreciate how the economic system creates new gains and losses; those who lack this appreciation will favor "fair" [i.e., ex post] treatment of the parties [Easterbrook, 1984:12].

With respect to the litigation of environmental and natural resource questions, and ultimately the legal relations governing society, the point is that one must be careful, that no matter how fair or just a particular decision may appear upon immediate application (under ex post scrutiny), the particular decision may serve to structure incentives in such a way that it generates significant future costs (revealed through ex ante analysis). The lesson is not to truncate analysis one way or the other, but instead to examine the created incentives and weigh the benefits and the costs, both long term and short term.

(2) Open and Closed Systems

Before leaving this chapter, it helps to relax one of the assumptions made earlier -- that of looking at a nation state in a closed setting. We can slightly revise Figure III.2 and look at a nation state in an open economy. Figure III.3 attempts to capture the additional flows that one needs to consider once the closed system assumption is relaxed.

What we observe here is that a nation state in an open system can attenuate some of the pressures on the ecological integrity of its own natural environment. Within an open system, a nation state can take a variety of actions which may have either positive or negative impacts on its own or its neighbor's economy and environment. First, a nation could export its natural resources for its own financial gain thereby enhancing its per capita GNP; second, it could import natural resources for production purposes. The extent to which the nation already owns a particular resource, importing more from other nations would serve to diminish the extraction rates from its own resource pools. Third, a nation could also expand its imports of finished goods and thereby avoid some of the negative externalities associated with the "in-house," material transformation, that is, the production processes necessary to produce the nation's goods. Fourth, a nation might export goods again for its financial gain. Finally, a nation could elect to export its residuals. That is, instead of depositing the residuals of production and consumption back into its own natural system, in an attempt to preserve its own environment, a nation may elect to export them to other countries.

a. Spaceship Earth -- As should be evident, the conceptual model raises many more questions when one thinks not of one nation in an open system, but all of the nations on one earth -- the phenomena of the so-called *spaceship earth* (Boulding, 1966). Kenneth Boulding perceived an open system as a "cowboy economy", the cowboy being symbolic of the illimitable plains and also associated with reckless, exploitative, romantic, and violent behavior. In the cowboy economy, consumption and production are regarded as a good thing. If there are infinite resources (inputs) and infinite reservoirs where effluents and emissions can be deposited, then the "throughput" (production and consumption) are good measures of the well-being of society. However, if the earth is not open but closed, it would then be regarded as a "spaceship" with a spaceship economy. Viewed from this vantage point, extraction and pollution place significant limits on the throughput. As in a spaceship, consumption and production must be minimized not maximized. The measure of success is no longer the largest level of consumption or highest output but the sustainability of the earth inhabitants on the spaceship with that sustainability a function of the nature, extent, quality, and

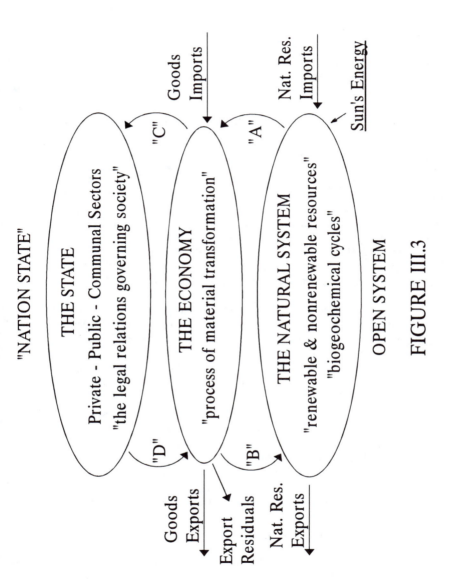

"NATION STATE"

THE STATE

Private - Public - Communal Sectors

"the legal relations governing society"

THE ECONOMY

"process of material transformation"

THE NATURAL SYSTEM

"renewable & nonrenewable resources"

"biogeochemical cycles"

OPEN SYSTEM

"C"

"A"

"D"

"B"

Goods Imports

Nat. Res. Imports

Sun's Energy

Goods Exports

Export Residuals

Nat. Res. Exports

FIGURE III.3

complexity of the stock of resources as well as how the residuals are treated. Figure III.4 is intended to capture the basic elements of the spaceship earth.

Within Figure III.4 it is evident that there is no "World Government," but instead hundreds of individual nation-states with each nation state having its own primary goals regarding economic growth and development and typically maintaining secondary goals (if any) regarding the ecological integrity of its ecosystems. To state the obvious, there are no "external" goods and services to be imported to the spaceship; there are no "external" factors of production to be imported to earth (except solar energy); and, while a nation's residuals can be transported from one nation to another nation, for all intents and purposes, they remain on earth and affect some nation's ecosystems (if not their own). What then is to be done once one recognizes that the quality of life aboard the spaceship is directly affected not only by enhancing the flow rates of the economic system, but that it is also impacted by the degradation of the life-supporting ecosystems, especially the biogeochemical flow rates inherent within the ecological systems? Since Boulding presentation of "spaceship earth," two different approaches have evolved to look at the many questions raised by this perspective -- the steady-state economy and sustainable development.

b. Steady-State Economics -- Herman Daly and Nicholas Georgescu-Roegen added much robustness to the fundamental concepts inherent in the spaceship earth in the literature formalizing the steady state economy.[6] The concept of the steady-state economy rests on an understanding of the Second Law of Thermodynamics or the Entropy Law. This law, simply stated, says that a closed system left at rest tends to deteriorate. Entropy can be seen as a measure of disorder. Two simple examples help underscore the issue before us -- oil and iron ore. Initially, in the ground crude oil is in a highly concentrated, ordered state (low entropy). As it is extracted and distilled and made into motor oil, it is transformed into a state of even lower entropy. However, as it is used up in the production and consumption sectors of the economy it dissipates into a highly disorganized entropic state never to be used again. Similarly iron ore in the ground is in a low entropic state. As it is extracted and formed into steel ingots it moves to an even lower entropic state. As in this case of oil, as steel is used throughout the economy in the form of various steel products, it does gradually get spread across the landscape increasing its entropic state. However, unlike oil, with additional inputs of energy resources (often associated with recycling efforts), the entropic process of steel can be reversed. Whereas energy cannot be created nor destroyed and thus goes from a higher to a lower quality level, the entopic processes of matter can be reversed but only with additional inputs of energy. Georgescu-Roegen (1980, 1971) and others applied this law to economics and concluded that, over time, production and consumption represent

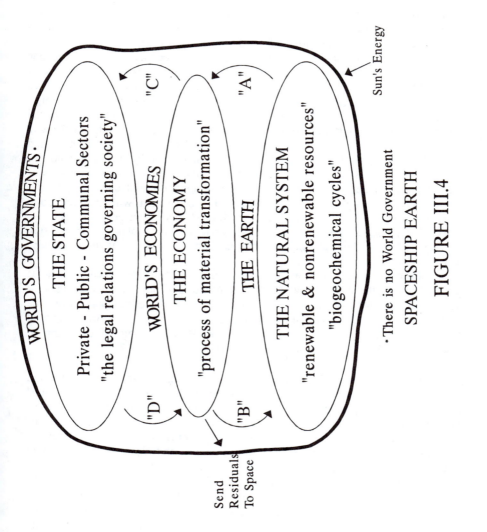

FIGURE III.4

a transformation of *valuable natural resources* to *valueless waste*. In most Western economies, both energy resources and material resources deteriorate -- the former because of the entropy law, the latter by choice.

Relying on the law of entropy, the steady-state economy is defined as one with constant stocks of people and artifacts (i.e., physical capital) maintained at some desired, sufficient levels. These stocks would be maintained by low rates of maintenance throughput, that is, the lowest feasible flows of matter and energy from the first stage of production (depletion of low-entropy materials from the environment) to the last stage of consumption (pollution of the environment with high-entropy wastes and exotic materials (Daly, 1977:17). The structure and order (low entropy) of the economic system is maintained by imposing a cost of disorder on the ecosystem. Since the entropy increase in the ecosystem is greater than the entropy decrease in the economy, as stock and maintenance throughput grow, the increasing disorder exported to the ecosystem will at some point interfere with its ability to provide natural goods and services to the society. Accordingly, an optimum stock is defined as one for which total service (the sum of services from the economy and the ecosystem) is at a maximum (Daly, 1977:34-35).

In this context, the thrust of natural resource and environmental policy is directly tied to the maintenance of a constant stock of physical wealth (capital) and a constant stock of people (population). Given the desired population, the focus of the steady-state economy becomes one attenuating the flow of throughput to maintain the population by imposing controls on the rate of depletion of resources, particularly nonrenewable resources (Daly, 1980:17).

c.   Sustainable Development[7] -- The conviction inherent within the concept of sustainable development is that generally, economic development must consider both (1) protection of natural resources and (2) the maintenance of environmental quality -- that is both flow "A" and flow "B." The concept of sustainable development springs from three intellectual sources: (1) the work in the ecological sciences; (2) the work in economics; and (3) work in philosophy and ethics. The concept of sustainable development is not a settled issue; it is perceived differently by people with different interests and different agendas.

There are two *general* definitions of sustainable development. First is the constrained economic growth definition, and second, is the maintenance-of-the-resource definition. Each deserves some elaboration. The constrained economic growth definition of sustainable development is taken to mean the pursuit of economic growth (as measured by GNP) subject to environmental constraints. It is seen as a two-staged process. First, the establishment of some contractual arrangement, incorporating ecological principles and environmental ethics to establish the "rules" that apply in formulating development policies; and second, within those established rules, the maximization of utility in the economic sense. The quest is for what may be termed -- the "right" incentives; the "right" technologies; and the "right" prices to internalize negative environmental externalities.

Alternatively, there is the maintenance-of-the-resource definition of sustainable development. Generally, this view disdains and rejects the two-staged process of the constrained economic growth advocates. They argue that "well-being" is not the same as "well-having" and that nature is to be respected and not exploited for production of inputs and outputs -- the emphasis is on "enoughness" in the context of reduced rates of economic growth -- especially for the developed nations.

To be more precise it should be noted that within this definition, there are two themes. Theme 1 takes a preservation ecocentric position. Here the emphasis is on the need for severe constraints on economic growth within an idealized decentralized socioeconomic system. Theme 2 represents an extreme preservationist or the "deep ecology" position. Here the emphasis is on the rights for nonhuman species.

Notwithstanding these nuances between and among advocates of sustainable development, as described by Sandra Batie, in general it is safe to say that the maintenance-of-the-resource advocates take the following positions:

● perceive that the biosphere imposes limits on economic growth,

● express a lack of faith in either science or technology as leading to human betterment,

● support redistributive justice and egalitarian ethics,

● profess concern over population growth and have faith in the wisdom of human capital development, and

● have survival of species and protection of the environment and of minority cultures, rather than economic growth per se, as goals.

Whether the future will see either the constrained economic growth definition or the maintenance-of-the-resource definition of sustainable development become the new conventional wisdom is an open question. Of even greater interest is what ultimate impact each might have on both the economy and the environment -- both near term and long term.

(4) The Polarized Debate

Discussions (perhaps disputes) regarding solutions to environmental and natural resource problems are often polarized. One of the reasons stems from the baseline perspectives from which one joins the debate. That is, individuals enter the environmental debate typically as part of an entrenched interest group and bring to the table the underlying -- market oriented, steady-state, or sustainable -- ideology of some interest group. Thus, in attempting to unravel just who is on what side of which natural resource or environmental issue, one should always keep in mind the old bureaucratic adage "where one stands depends upon where one sits." Richard Lecomber has described two polar points of view -- the Pessimists and the Optimists -- that go a long way in capturing what ideologies one can find in economic and non-economic debates over natural resource and environmental questions. Perhaps it is better to refer to these two points of view as *non-economic* and *economic*. After carefully cautioning us that no one party of interest or contributor to the literature on environmental or natural resource economics will fall wholly within one point of view or the other, he went on to describe each.

a. The Non-Economic Point of View -- The advocates of the non-economic position emphasize the finiteness of the world and the limits this places on economic output. They go on to insist on the eventual necessity of a stationary state, when all output is derived from renewable resources. Moreover, they consider that severe resource scarcity is imminent and that many non-renewable resources are approaching exhaustion; that renewable resources (and environmental sinks) are being fully used and in many cases over-used. They emphasize the suddenness of the onset of scarcity and the consequent difficulties of adaptation; they are very skeptical of the adequacy of existing mechanisms, especially the market mechanism, to cope with such scarcity. They fear that, in the absence of a carefully planned adaptation to the stationary state, non-renewable resources will be exhausted suddenly and renewable resources will be overworked, with disastrous effects. According to Lecomber, the non-economic position advocates an across-the-board approach, for example zero economic growth. They often blame the materialistic and expansionist ethics of capitalist (as well as former communist) societies and the false optimism of the opposite camp for preventing the taking of necessary measures to avert disaster. They are skeptical of the power of technology to obviate or even significantly postpone the crisis. Lecomber also notes that some writers even see technology as hastening and aggravating the crisis. In one form or another nearly all emphasize the central role of population growth on aggravating the resource crisis; those who advocate the economic position share this view, thus is not a distinguishing characteristic (Lecomber, 1979:1-6).

b. The Economic Point of View -- In contrast, advocates of the economic position admit the physical finiteness of the would but question its significance. Some deny the eventual necessity of an end to economic growth and all question whether such an end is imminent. According to Lecomber, they argue that the physical measures of scarcity frequently quoted by advocates of the non-economic position are misleading in that they ignore new discoveries, substitution possibilities (between resources and, more significantly, man-made capital resources) and technical progress. They point out how, historically, resource scares have been averted in precisely this way. They emphasize the role of the price mechanism in stimulating the necessary adjustments (and, incidentally, believe that, if and when resource limits to growth do materialize, the price mechanism will play a central role in adaption to the stationary state). They believe, more positively, that the price mechanism allocates resource use reasonably well between different time periods. They admit the great uncertainty that must surround the distant future, but they tend to use this uncertainty to justify a short planning horizon. They are scornful of non-economic approaches to resource scarcity, particularly zero economic growth, which they see as unnecessary if not harmful to conservation, besides aggravating unemployment and the distribution of income. Optimists concede problems, even serious problems, when ownership rights are inadequately defined or externalities are present, for here the market mechanism on which they place such emphasis clearly fails; specific remedies directed to specific problems are indicated (Lecomber, 1979:1-6).

Many disciplines may help in attempting to formulate remedies to bring the *state*, the *economy*, and the *natural system* into a harmony that helps preserve the ecological integrity of a unique natural system. Before moving forward with the final two chapters, the reader should understand that the following material employs the analytical tools of conventional microeconomics and with this, comes closer to the view set forth by the economic perspective outlined above. This is not to suggest that the other views are less valuable, but in accordance with the goal set forth for this book in Chapter I, the remaining chapters are intended to provide the reader with the several contributions towards fashioning remedies based on economic theory.

ENDNOTES

1. The three stages of choice outlined here were originally presented in Mercuro and Ryan,(1984:13-42). They were also latter revised into their present form in Mercuro, 1989:1-26. For alternative formulations of the nexus among rights, institutions, and economic performance see Barzel,(1989); North,(1990); and Schmid,(1987).

2. The initial notion of status rights was developed and presented in Dales,(1972:152-154).

3. Kaldor-Hicks efficiency -- the so-called compensation principle in economics -- implies that society should adopt those legal changes that as a result of the change (a) income could have been redistributed after the change in the law so as to make everyone better off than before, and also that (b) it was not possible to improve welfare before the legal change took place simply by redistributing income. A straight forward analysis is provided in Price,(1977:19-30), while a more detailed explanation is presented in Feldman,(1980:138-149).

4. See Hardin,(1968).

5. This matter is fully explored in Brandl and Bungert,(1992).

6. Many of their original ideas are contained in Daly (1980) and Daly (1977); see also Pirages (1977) as well as Olson and Landsberg (1973).

7. This section borrows directly from Batie,(1989).

REFERENCES

Alchian A.A. and Demsetz, H. 1973. The Property Rights Paradigm. *Journal of Economic History* 33 (March): 16-27.

Batie, S.S. 1989. Sustainable Development: Challenges to the Profession of Agricultural Economics. *American Journal of Agricultural Economics* 71 (December): 1083-1101.

Barzel, Y. 1989. *Economic Analysis of Property Rights*. Cambridge: Cambridge University Press.

Boulding, K. 1966. The Economics of the Coming Spaceship Earth. In *Environmental Quality in a Growing Economy*, ed. H. Jarrett. Baltimore: Johns Hopkins University Press: 3-14.

Brandl E. and Bungert, H. 1992. Constitutional Entrenchment of Environmental Protection: A Comparative Analysis of Experiences Abroad. *Harvard Environmental Law Review* 16 (No.1): 1-100.

Coleman, J.S. 1974. *Power and the Structure of Society*. New York: W.W. Norton and Company.

Daly, H.E. ed. 1980. *Economics, Ecology and Ethics: Essays Toward a Steady-State Economy*. San Francisco: W.H. Freeman and Co.

Daly, H.E. 1977. *Steady-State Economics*. San Francisco: W.H. Freeman and Co.

Dales, J.H. 1972. Rights in Economics. In *Perspectives on Property*, ed. G. Wunderlich and W.L. Gibson. University Park, PA: Institute for Research on Land and Water Resources, Pennsylvania State University: 149-155.

Easterbrook F.H. 1984. Forward: The Court and the Economic System. *Harvard Law Review* 98 (4): 4-60.

Feldman, A.M. 1980. *Welfare Economics and Social Choice Theory*. Boston: Martinus Nijhoff Publishing.

Georgescu-Roegen, N. 1980. "The Entropy Law and the Economic Problem. In *Economics, Ecology, Ethics: Essays Toward a Steady-State Economy*, ed. H. Daly, 49-60. San Francisco: W.H. Freeman and Company.

Georgescu-Roegen, N. 1971. *The Entropy Law and the Economic Process*. Cambridge, MA: Harvard University Press.

Hardin, G. 1968. The Tragedy of the Commons. *Science* 162 (December 13th): 1243-1248.

Lecomber, R. 1979. *The Economics of Natural Resources*. New York: John Wiley and Sons.

Mercuro, N. 1989. Towards a Comparative Institutional Approach to the Study of Law and Economics. In *Law and Economics*, ed. N. Mercuro. Boston: Kluwer Academic Publishing: 1-26.

Mercuro, N. and Ryan, T. 1984. *Law Economics and Public Policy*. Greenwich, CT: JAI Press.

North, D.C. 1990. *Institutions, Institutional Change and Economic Performance*. Cambridge: Cambridge University Press.

Olson, M. and Landsberg, H.H. eds. 1973. *The No-Growth Society*. New York: W.W. Norton and Co.

Pirages, D.C. ed. 1977. *The Sustainable Society*. New York: Praeger Publishing.

Price, C.M. 1977. *Welfare Economic in Theory and Practice*. London: Macmillian Press Ltd.

Randall, A. 1981. *Resource Economics*. Columbus: Grid Publishing Inc.

Schmid, A.A. 1987. *Power, Property, and Public Choice*. New York: Praeger Publishing.

Stokes, K.M. 1992. *Man and the Biosphere: Toward a Coevolutionary Political Economy*. Armonk, N.Y.: M.E. Sharpe.

Ullmann, W. 1966. *The Individual and Society in the Middle Ages*, Baltimore: Johns Hopkins University Press.

CHAPTER IV

THE ECONOMICS OF NATURAL RESOURCES

INTRODUCTION

The past decades have brought with them enormous changes. With these changes have come issues of great concern, especially the implications of conserving and preserving natural resources for human welfare. In this chapter we discuss the optimal rate of resource utilization in the context of economic theory.

The economic approach asserts that the cause of natural resource problems or environmental problems is neither the primacy of humans over nature nor warped values but an imperfect translation of values into actions. Therefore, any solution will rest on institutional changes that alter human behavior so as to make it more conducive to ecological preservation. This is decidedly an anthropocentric view, but as John R. Williams affirms:

> It does not follow from this, of course, that humanity can or should with impunity do whatsoever it wills to its biological environment. Nor -- obviously -- does it follow that one generation can or should act in ways to imperil the well-being of the planet that later generations will receive from its hand. It does, however, at least suggest that a sense of perspective is required (Williams, 1992:4).

When individual choices differ from collective choices the problem is not one of values, but the decision making process by which the choices are reached.

(1) Neither Costs Nor Benefits Are Infinite

It must be underscored that while there are many difficulties in determining the dollar value of the benefits and the costs associated with abating pollution --*they are typically neither zero nor infinite*. The recent attempts (1) to value renewable and nonrenewable resources and (2) to value the benefits of the abatement of environmental pollution are reviewed in this chapter. As will become evident in this and the next chapter, the theory of the simple analytics of natural resource and environmental economics assumes that accurate estimates of the costs as well as the benefits of pollution abatement can be made. We are well aware that, especially with respect to the latter, such quantitative estimates are often difficult to acquire. However, we believe that while that work continues, it remains absolutely essential to move forward with the theoretical work that underlies the formulation of legal-economic based remedies.

As explored in Chapter III, there are pervasive difficulties in predicting the impact of various residuals on ecosystems and the cumulative effects of extractive activities. These difficulties stem from several sources. First, the synergistic effects of the simultaneous emission of several residuals into an ecosystem -- the impact can often be more severe than the mere linear addition of the impacts of each individual source. Second, the determination of the threshold levels of the ability of ecosystems to either absorb environmental wastes or to fend off the ecological disruptions associated with excessive extractions. Finally, the fact that the time horizons associated with ecological systems are often very long -- much longer than those inherent in the market. It may take decades for a an ecological problem to manifest itself (Dietz and van der Straaten, 1992:32-34).

(2) The Evaluation of Nature as an Asset

The economic approach attempts to maximize the value of natural resources by creating a balance between the preservation and the use of an asset. An asset is a good that produces a stream of benefits (aesthetic, financial or recreational) over time. This balance can only be achieved by valuing the various flows of service received including the negative effects of using the environment.

There is no perfect way to evaluate the net social benefits of natural resources. All methods of quantification, as we will see, have some advantages and shortcomings. Furthermore, some benefits as well as damages may be impossible to quantify and equally impossible to value. Economists have yet to design a method to quantify the value of entire ecosystems or the value of an animal species for its own sake. There are no possible ways to assign values to traditional ways of life like those of the Amazonian Indians or Australian aborigines.

(3) Detecting Resource Scarcity

The very essence of economics pertains to the allocation of scarce resources for competing ends. According to neoclassical economics, prices are signals about relative scarcities, costs of production, and/or changes in consumers preferences. It is important to ascertain if the prices generated by market forces are sufficient to indicate the seriousness and imminence of a resource scarcity. If the price system (we have seen in Chapter I how prices are distorted by externalities) cannot provide signals *on time*, society must look into some other means for detecting scarcity.

According to Tom Tietenberg (1992:338), a good indicator must possess the following characteristics: (1) it must be forward looking, i.e., it is not sufficient to indicate that a scarcity occurred but that it is about to occur; (2) it must allow for comparisons so as to determine the seriousness of the scarcity relative to the availability of substitutes; and (3) it must be quantifiable so that calculation can be readily made from available information. No indicator, at the present time, has all of these three properties so until one is developed, we must rely on the following five.

a. Physical Indicators -- A reserve-to-use ratio computes the time that it would take for an existing stock of a resource to be depleted or exhausted at the prevailing rate of use. These ratios are static and assumed fixed. They may be applied for depletable resources, but are meaningless for the treatment of renewable resources. The outstanding feature of reserve-to-use ratios is that they can be easily calculated from available data. Such ratios can also be useful for comparisons to determine priorities, however, it must be noted that they are misleading for forecasting purposes.

b. Resource Prices -- Despite the problems of externalities, resource prices are fairly good carriers of information. Current price levels and relative prices reflect expectations of consumers and producers about the future course of a resource. They are affected by rising demand, possibilities of stock augmentation and substitution, and changes in the cost of extraction.   In addition to externalities, when prices are distorted by government price controls, regulations, artificial subsidies, and even "false" expectations (speculative bubbles) the information carried by them cannot be relied upon. The ability of market prices to forecast the future depends entirely upon the ability of market participants to anticipate future substitution possibilities, technological changes, demand patterns and so on. Only to the extent that market participants can forecast such events can market prices be regarded as good indicators.

c. Ricardian or Scarcity Rent -- David Ricardo, a prominent classical economist, interpreted *rent* as return to differential soil qualities. As lower quality land was brought into production, the superior quality land earned an additional profit strictly due to the difference in quality. Hence, as lower and lower quality soil is brought into production more and more rent is accrued to the *owners* of the better soil quality. A tenant of good land must sell products at a price that is sufficiently high to cover costs -- labor, capital, and management -- as well as the rent for the use of the land. If the price is not high enough the land will not be cultivated. The last soil to be used will be that which has zero rent. It must be emphasized that the landlord receives an income only because he owns the land. When land (or any resource) is held in common property there is no rent. Ricardian or scarcity rent changes according to the forward vision of the owner of the resource. Only when the owner perceives that the resource is becoming more scarce will the expected rent be higher. In some ways, scarcity rent is a better indicator than price.

For example, if the price of wheat falls it may be erroneously concluded that it is due to higher yields (less scarce land) when in fact land was getting more scarce. The reduction in the price of wheat may be due to lower transportation and distribution costs. If the reduction in these costs is larger than the increases in rent one could infer the wrong conclusion. If marginal costs of resource utilization are constant, scarcity rent is a good indicator, that is, the higher the rent the higher the scarcity. However, if marginal costs increase, less of the resource will be utilized and scarcity rent will *decline,* leading to a wrong conclusion.

d. Marginal Discovery Cost -- When scarcity rent is not observable, the additional costs involved in the discovery of new resources or resource substitutes can be used instead. The higher the marginal discovery costs the greater the scarcity.

e. Marginal Extraction Cost -- When society begins to utilize lower quality or inferior resources more and more inputs (capital, labor) are needed for extraction. This increase of inputs per unit resource extracted is reflected in higher extraction costs. A fall over time in input costs per unit of extracted resource suggests that either new, low-cost sources have been discovered, or that technological progress has reduced the amount of capital and labor required to extract the resource. An index of wages, salaries, and interest rates can be constructed to represent input costs. Because increasing marginal costs reflect a greater scarcity, such an index is a good indicator regardless of the structure of ownership, particularly for common property resources such as whales and fish.

The main drawback of this indicator is its backward looking nature. As with the reserve-to-use indicator, the index of marginal extraction costs are computed *ex-post*, i.e., it does not provide information about future scarcities.

Current observations of higher marginal extraction costs allow governments and market participants only to react rather than to act in anticipation of the scarcity.

(4) Dynamic Efficiency: The Maximization of the Net Present Value at the Margin

An ordinary factor of production differs from an exhaustible resource by the fact that the latter is limited in quantity and is not reproducible. Extraction and consumption of a unit today implies an *opportunity cost*: the value that may be obtained at some future date. A first condition for optimal depletion requires that price be equal to marginal costs. A second condition describes the path of this opportunity cost over time. For example, an oil reservoir has a limited amount of petroleum. The owner of the reservoir has the choice of extracting all of it today or leaving some for future extraction. Assume that the marginal costs of extraction are zero. If the owner extracts all the oil today, the revenues can be deposited into a bank account to earn interest. Alternatively, if the price of oil tomorrow is expected to increase at a rate higher than the interest rate it would be better for the owner to leave the oil in the ground. Therefore, as long as the expected rate of increase in price of an exhaustible resource is higher than or equal to the rate of return foregone it will be more efficient for the owner to leave the extraction for tomorrow.

a. Maximization of Present Value -- Present value is defined as the equivalent value today of a future quantity of money. Thus, if the interest rate is 10 per cent per year, a person would be indifferent -- if asked to choose -- between having 1.00 dollar today or 1.10 a year from now. The present value of the future 1.10 dollars is 1. If 1.00 dollar is left for two periods it will *compound* to 1.21 [1 x (1+0.10) x (1+0.10) = (1+0.10)^2]. In this case the present value of 1.21 to be received in two years will be 1.00 dollar. The present value thus *discounts* the interest rate to be accumulated during the time under consideration. The present value (PV) of a single payment can be calculated by the following formula:

(1) $$PV[B_n] = \frac{B_n}{(1+r)^n}$$

where B_n is the payment, r is the interest rate and n is the number of periods in the future.

When there are two or more payments in the future, the present value of a stream of payments is computed according to the following formula:

$$PV[B_0, B_1, ..., B_n] = B_0 + \frac{B_1}{(1+r)} + \frac{B_2}{(1+r)^2} + ... + \frac{B_n}{(1+r)^n}$$

(2)

$$\text{or} \quad \sum_{i=0}^{n} \frac{B_i}{(1+r)^i}$$

where B_o, B_1, ... , B_n is the payment made at the *ith* period. The present value is found by *discounting* each payment for its corresponding time periods.

> *An allocation of resources across n time periods is dynamically efficient if it maximizes the present value of the net benefits that could be received from all the possible ways of allocating those resources over the n periods.*

The following example illustrates the case of dynamic efficiency using two periods and an interest rate of 10 per cent. Assume that the demand for an exhaustible resource X is given by $P = 8 - 0.4Q_x$ and it is constant for both periods, the marginal cost of extracting the resource is $2 per unit. If the supply is more than 30 for both periods (see Figure IV.1) there will be enough to satisfy the demand (at 15 units per period) at the price of $2 per unit *regardless of the interest rate*. This would imply the resource is *not depletable* in two periods. However, if the supply is less than 30 across both periods, the resource will be depleted in two periods. How is the use of the resource maximized?

According to the dynamic efficiency criterion, consider the value of consuming 15 units in the first period (with a corresponding price of $2 [panel a]) and 5 units in the second period (with a price of $6 [panel b]). Such an allocation of consumption provides net benefits of 45 [Panel (a), shaded area A] in the first period and 25 in the second period [Panel (b), shaded area B][1]. The present value of net benefits for the first period is 45. For the second period, the present value is found by discounting the 10% interest [25/(1 + 0.1) = 22.73]. Thus the total present value of allocating 15 units today and 5 units next period is $67.73. We can continue using different allocations until the *maximum* value is found.

b. Maximization of Present Value over Several Periods -- Mathematically, a maximum exists when the present value of the marginal net benefit for period one is equal to the present value of the marginal net benefit for period 2. If there are more than two periods the condition states that a maximum is reached when the present value of the marginal net benefit is equal for each and every period[2].

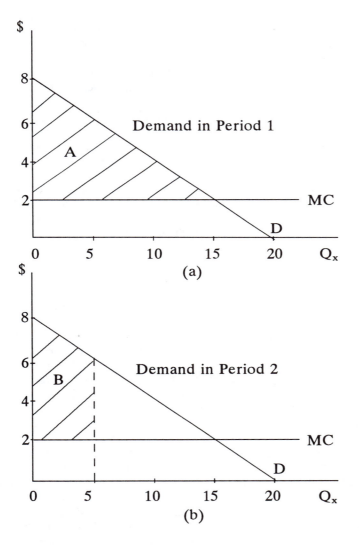

FIGURE IV.1

Intuitively, if the present value of additional net benefits in period X is higher than the present value of additional net benefits in period Y, total net benefits will increase by extracting more in period X than in period Y. If the additional net benefits diminish with increased extraction (as is the usual case) extraction will continue until the additional net benefits are exhausted (i.e., net benefits will have reached a maximum). This is similar to the *equiproportional value* principle applied throughout economic theory[3].

c. The Sustainability Criterion -- The dynamic efficiency criterion is applicable to any institutional setting. It is equally suitable for a dictatorship or for democratic capitalism. However, it says nothing about the rights of future generations for the resource. The fact that an exhaustible resource is "efficiently depleted" does not address the question whether the resource should be entirely consumed by present or near-present generations[4]. We will discuss the intergenerational problem when we discuss the discount rate.

(5) The Measuring of Benefits

In theory, the maximization principle is straight-forward. However, in the real world the valuation of benefits, costs, the interest rate, and the uncertainty surrounding these values requires the availability of a substantial amount of reliable information. The basic economic approach is the *trade off* principle. Individuals compare competing means to obtain a goal. Thus benefits and costs can be measured by observing what goods or activities are *foregone*. The alternatives available are good estimators of costs and benefits when direct measurement is not possible. Benefits of these alternatives can be measured by demand estimation, incremental action, willingness-to-pay surveys, and/or comparisons with similar operations.

a. Demand Estimation -- Benefits provided by a resource give rise to demand. When the benefits are tangible and indivisible (private goods) the demand curve provides an accurate measure of the willingness and ability of the user of the resource to pay a certain price. However, when there are external benefits or the good is a public good, that estimate of demand does not measure benefits correctly. As previously indicated (in Chapter I), external benefits accruing to third persons result in a persistent under-utilization of resources.

For the empirical estimation of demand, the investigator gathers a set of quantities consumed at different prices as well as other variables that may affect the demand. A mathematical function is assumed and through statistical techniques the "best" fit is chosen. This technique is excellent for private goods because there usually is a market for them. Since there are no markets for most public goods, their demand must be inferred in a different way.

b.   Incremental Action -- The estimation of benefit time paths for recreational facilities or preservation relative to development is a more difficult task to undertake. As income increases the demand for preservation increases, hence, development initially is more valuable than preservation. However, as development raises level of income the value of preservation increases. Equilibrium will exist when the marginal value of preservation and the marginal value of development are the same. An equilibrium solution can be observed by incremental action. This method consists of increasing either activity by a small amount; usually development, because it is initially more valuable than preservation. If the additional benefits of development have a small or negligible effect on recreational benefits then additional development occur. Development should stop as soon it becomes detrimental to preservation.   Obviously, *incremental* action estimates are not possible when decisions cannot be made in small amounts.

c.   Contingent Valuation and Surveys -- When there is no market for a good either because it is a private good (*nonrival* good) or because externalities distort the market price, the valuation of benefits can be elicited by placing consumers in a hypothetical scenario. They will be asked how much they would be *willing-to-pay* (WTP) for the public good, the abatement of a negative externality, or an amenity.   There is a growing acceptance among economists about the validity of this method (Passell, 1993:20).

The *Contingent Valuation Method* (CVM) (Mitchell and Carson, 1992) consists of asking a random sample of households how much would they be willing to pay to obtain a clearly defined "amount" of a public good or how much would they be willing to accept (WTA) in compensation for some "bads" or risks. The CVM does not require that a "quantifiable" amount be defined, only that the characteristics of how the public good will be supplied, under different scenarios, be described with clarity. This method of estimating demand has two obvious drawbacks: the individual may (1) not know how to respond if actually faced with such a hypothetical scenario; and (2) know but not tell the truth.   When the consumer is familiar and has experience with the product or project, comparative studies have shown that the CVM is valid and reliable in estimating the valuation of benefits (Dickie, *et. al.*, 1987).

The validity and reliability of the responses depend upon the description of the scenario, the perception of the respondent as to how the answer will influence the supply of the good, the expectations of the respondent regarding the payment method, and the obligation to pay.   The description of the good is, perhaps, the most critical factor for the validity of the survey. It must provide a detailed description of the good and the circumstances under which it will be supplied. The supply scenario must be as plausible as possible. It must indicate the minimum amount to be supplied, the physical and institutional structure of the supply, possible or potential substitutes, and the payment method. Biases in the estimation of the true WTP occur when there is *strategic behavior*. For example, if the respondent perceives that the good will be provided regardless of the answer and expects an obligation to pay a lump-sum, the bid will be a quantity lower than the true WTP. If the respondent perceives that the answer will influence the decision and wants to force the decision on others the bid will be a quantity higher than the true WTP. When the respondents are certain the good will be provided anyway and believe there will be no connection between their answers and what will actually be charged they are likely to answer any quantity, without making any effort to study the true value of their preferences. There are several ways to detect and correct for strategic behavior:

● If the number of refusals is high or if there is a significant number of *protest answers* (such as zero or very high), it is likely that the description of the scenario is not a very good one or the interviewer is asking the question the wrong way.

● Additional information can be provided so that the respondents have an opportunity to change their mind. If this elicits significantly different answers, there is a high probability of the presence of strategic behavior.

● If a comparison of the hypothetical answer with the actual payment for similar services shows a large discrepancy the answers are likely to be biased.

● If the use of sub-samples and pre-tests show significantly different answers the validity of the survey is questionable.

In order to avoid strategic behavior, the questionnaire must: (1) clearly define the scenario for the supply of the public good, the abatement of the negative externality, or the amenity; (2) impress upon the respondents that their answer will influence the decision to supply the good; (3) convince the respondents that they will be obligated to pay; (4) describe clearly the method of payment; and (5) state that there will be a connection between the amount of the good provided and the quantity charged for the good.

There are several ways to elicit the willingness-to-pay using contingent valuation surveys. They range from open questions to a simple *take-it-or-leave-it* proposition. Other variables such as income, size of family, education, monthly expenditures on similar goods, household satisfaction with similar services, etc., are incorporated in the questionnaire.

(i) *Bidding* -- This method resembles the way economists describe demand. A respondent is asked to bid for different quantities of the good.

Sometimes the procedure consists of a combination of "yes/no" questions and a direct open-ended question to elicit the maximum WTP. This question format is called an "abbreviated bidding procedure with follow-up." The initial price has a significant influence on the answers (Whitington, *et. al.*, 1993) because it gives the respondent an indication of how much others value the good. To determine the significance of this problem several starting values are chosen. If the median or mean response is not significantly different for each initial point, the method is accepted.

(ii) *Payment card* -- In this method, the respondent is shown a card with different combination of quantities and prices. The enumerator describes each of the relevant options by reading from a prepared text, or in some cases, by showing diagrams or pictures to the respondents. This method does not have the starting point bias but it is more difficult to design.

(iii) *Take-it-or-leave* -- This is a single question with a yes/no option. The investigators design different values for different respondents. The median answer is taken to be the WTP for the average consumer (the median represents the 50th percentile of all answers). This method is simpler to design and to administer. The median WTP is found by econometric methods called LOGIT or PROBIT.

d. Hedonic Pricing -- Another way to determine the willingness to pay is to measure it indirectly through actual market prices. The value of amenities (such as the structural features of a house, its interior space, freedom from aircraft noise, nearness to schools, air and water quality, etc.) cannot be evaluated separately, however, they do command a price in the market. The value of each characteristic is incorporated in the total price. Hedonic pricing is a technique developed to separate the willingness to pay for each characteristic (McMillan, 1979:174-187).

An indirect evaluation of the benefits of prevention can be obtained by measuring how much individuals are willing to pay to live in houses free of pollution or how much higher salaries must be for people to engage in dangerous occupations, all other things being equal. A surprising result is that the methods provide consistent and similar valuations. For example, the survey method shows a person in the Los Angeles area will be willing to pay $30 for a 30% improvement in air quality; the housing market approach shows an average expense of $40 to obtain a similar level of air quality (Freeman, 1979:152-173).

The hedonic pricing approach can also be used to measure intangibles, for example, recreational benefits. An estimator of the willingness of individuals to incur the cost to acquire such benefits can be used. According to Tietenberg (1992:76), the method developed essentially entails a survey of travel costs for visitors of recreational areas. When there is congestion, the technique underestimates the value of benefits (congestion reduces benefits by itself). The time path of benefits can be obtained through comparisons of utilization rates with similar facilities.

Sometimes benefits can be measured by the prevention of damages. Such is the case of pollution control. The benefits of pollution control can be measured directly by the reduction in health care costs or by the increase in soils' fertility, or indirectly by analyzing housing or labor markets.

(6) The Measuring of Costs

Economists differentiate between *accounting* and *opportunity* costs. Accounting costs are measurable and are explicit costs plus some implicit costs incurred in an activity. Opportunity costs are the foregone benefits of alternative resource use. The estimation of accounting costs is much easier than the evaluation of opportunity costs. The most appropriate way to estimate direct costs is the *engineering method*. In contrast, implicit costs are estimated by surveys, the willingness to pay, and comparisons with similar or related activities. The measuring of implicit costs is not different from the measuring of benefits using the methods presented earlier. Perhaps we should note that surveys tend to be biased depending upon the size and nature of the sample, the type and form of the questions, and the purpose of the survey. Hence, the results have to be carefully studied before any conclusions or recommendations are implemented.

In the engineering method, the available technologies are categorized according to capital (initial investment) costs (e.g., construction, acquisition, installation, operating and maintenance costs, etc.). All these costs are annualized, that is, the annual payments a firm would have to make if all funds were borrowed; these annualized costs are called the Equivalent Uniform Annual Costs (EUAC). The different alternatives are compared using the computed EUAC and the one with the lowest equivalent annual cost is chosen. There are various shortcomings to this method. First, only readily computable costs can be used; intangibles must be somehow converted to dollar terms; second, the interest rate for the "equivalency" is very subjective, and third, no estimate of the future is certain and "expected" values must be used. In order to minimize these shortcomings, *sensitivity analyses* are conducted. With the development of fast computers and electronic spreadsheets such as the well-known LOTUS 1-2-3 a sensitivity analysis is carried out by WHAT IF? questions. Different scenarios are then developed and critical variables or thresholds are determined.

(7) The Measuring of the Discount Rate

One of the most controversial variables in the determination of present value as well as for the computation of EUAC is the rate of interest. There are two definitions of interest rate in economics:

• The rate of time preference of consumption, that is, since individuals generally prefer to consume now rather than wait, the interest is the reward that a consumer gets for postponing consumption.

• The opportunity cost of capital. This cost arises because of: (1) the time needed to recover the investment; since the funds cannot be employed for some time--cal'ed maturity--the longer the maturity the higher the interest rate; (2) the risk involved in the activity or the probability that the investment will be profitable; the higher the risk the higher the interest rate; (3) the expected rate of inflation; since inflation lowers the purchasing power of money, in order to compensate the investment from any loss in value due to higher prices the interest rate must be higher.

Because the financial market is one of the most efficient markets in the sense that it moves in anticipation of future events, market interest rates for financial instruments of different maturities are good indicators of inflationary expectations and low-risk alternatives. Thus market rates plus a risk premium can be satisfactorily employed as the opportunity cost of capital. However, while these interest rates are valid for private investments and individual choices, they cannot be used for the determination of a *social discount rate*.

The evaluation of present value involves a calculation of the future stream of net benefits and a discount rate (see Equation (1), Section IV.4.a), the higher the discount rate the lower the present value. Therefore, the higher the discount rate the less valuable becomes the future stream of benefits. In particular, the higher the value of benefits assigned to future generations the lower the discount rate and vice-versa. Since consumption by future generations is a public good (present generations gain utility by the prospect of a progressive civilization) present market interest rates underestimate their value (Fisher, 1981:70). Therefore the social discount rate to be used for public projects must be lower than similar rates for private projects. There is no universal consensus as to how much lower the social discount should be. Agencies of the United States government are currently using 10 percent despite the fact that market interest rates are very low.

The existence of a "social" discount rate rests on the assumption of the additivity of intergenerational utilities. John Rawls (1971) challenged this view and proposed a *maximin criterion* to determine social welfare. According to this criterion a generation that adds to the capital stock has a claim to more retirement consumption provided by the labor of the next generation, which in turn has an obligation to work more in exchange for the added capital. This assumes that factors of production are substitutable, which is acceptable for renewable resources but it is questionable for depletable resources. Despite this drawback, the intergenerational *maximin* criterion is an alternative to the use of a social discount rate in the maximization of the present value of future net benefits.

(8) The Assessment of Risk

It is self-evident that any future estimates are uncertain and imprecise. Uncertainty necessarily implies risk. The assessment of risk involves:

- an evaluation of the probabilities of occurrence

- identification and quantification of risks

- an evaluation of how much risk is acceptable

With respect to the first, statistical methods have been developed to evaluate probabilities and *expected values*. Statistical methods allow the inference of a range of probabilities for the occurrence of a given variable.   The most elementary technique is the calculation of the expected value of the most likely occurrence and the uncertainty or dispersion of the variable around this expected value.   A weighted average or mean (μ) is an adequate measure of expected value, while the standard deviation (σ) or variance (σ^2) is a good estimator of dispersion. Obviously, the higher the dispersion the higher the uncertainty and the higher the risk.

The expected value E[x] for discrete outcomes is calculated by the following formula:

$$E[x] = x_1 p(x_1) + x_2 p(x_2) + x_3 p(x_3) + ... + x_n p(x_n)$$

(3) $$\text{or} \quad E[x] = \sum_{i=1}^{n} x_i p(x_i) \quad \text{and}$$

$$p(x_1) + p(x_2) + p(x_3) + ... + p(x_n) = 1$$

where x_i is outcome *ith* and $p(x_i)$ is the probability in percents of occurrence of the outcome x_i. When the outcomes are continuous, the expected value is calculated as follows:

(4)
$$E[x] = \int_{-\infty}^{\infty} x\, f(x)\, dx$$

where $f(x)$ is a probability distribution function, such as the Gaussian curve (better known as the normal distribution) that has a bell shape as in Figure IV.2 where two functions with different variances (risks) are depicted. Though both have the same expected value or average (μ) the taller one indicates that the average outcome involves lower risk, as indicated by the lower dispersion around the mean, that is, a lower standard deviation (σ).

Econometrics and applied statistics are at the forefront of economic knowledge, with an enormous range of applications and valid methods of risk assessment. Experiments or statistical data analysis can be conducted with different levels of sophistication (Chechile, 1991:64-91). The problem rests in the extrapolation of the findings and how much risk should society be willing to accept. Jay Lehr (1992) has proposed the concept of Life Lost Expectancy (LLE). All risk can be translated into lost expectancy. For example, if 1000 people at birth have a life expectancy of 70 years, the combined total is 70,000. Since we know that 14 people (out of the 1000) will die in an automobile accident at an average age of 35 years, when 14 is multiplied by 35 we have a loss of 490 years out of the 70,000. Subtracting the 490 from 70,000 and dividing by the original 1000 yields an average life expectancy is now 69½ or a LLE of 6 months due to automobile accidents. Corrections can be made for factors such as lowering the total number of people because the very young and very old do not drive. The LLE has been an imaginative way to calculate the impact of risky activities such as: smoking (LLE of 6.4 for men, 2.3 years for women), proper weight (2.5 years for every 30 pounds of overweight), coal mining (3 years), hurricanes and tornados (one day). Though averages do not matter for each individual person, they do matter in determining the spending of public money and in deciding how much risk society is willing to bear.

(9) Non-maximizing Evaluation

Not all evaluation techniques determine the optimum level of benefits or costs. Sometimes studies are carried out to determine the effect of actions on others, the environment, or individuals in society.

a. Impact Studies -- For any allocation to be useful, it must be carried out in an *optimum* way. This implies a systematic method for finding the lowest-cost means of accomplishing the objective. An *impact* analysis attempts to quantify the consequences of various actions. In contrast with the benefit/cost approach, an impact study does not necessarily optimize. It only attempts to provide

"unbiased and reliable" information to policy makers.

      b. The Value of Life -- A traditional way to measure the value of life involves the present value of future earnings. However, estimating the market value of an individual is extremely subjective and plagued with philosophical questions. The economic approach of *willingness to pay* has been used instead. For example, it can be estimated by the additional amount paid for better and safer automobiles, by consumer purchases of smoke detectors, life insurance, and homes in non-polluted areas, by choice of occupations and particularly, by how much consumers are willing to pay for the safety of their children (Tregarthen, 1990). The methodology has its shortcomings because it bases its estimates on averages. Thus little can be said with respect to the value of a particular individual. However, it has important consequences for public policy as well as for the court room. The courts may use these values as a benchmark for estimating compensation payments.

      The Life Lost Expectancy criterion can be very useful for the determination of the effectiveness of policy. The LLE method has been used to estimate the cost of policies. For example[5], the World Health Organization can save a life for $50 in Gambia, for $20 in Indonesia. A $550 investment saves one life from malaria in the Third World but $5000 is needed to save one through nutrition. The costs for one life in the developed countries are much higher. It costs $90,000 in cancer-screening to save the life of one woman. Blood pressure checks could save one life at a cost of $150,000. The assessment of risk and the acceptance of certain amounts of risk are important considerations in the evaluation of policies and for a judicious allocation of resources.

      c. Other methods[6] -- There are other ways to estimate how much risk society can bear such as *de minimis* risk, comparative risk, and risk-benefit analysis. Natural hazards are used as an indicator of a threshold of *de minimis* risk such as natural radiation or lightning strikes. If the risk or the probability is below this threshold then it is an acceptable level. Comparative-Risk Analysis (CRA) uses the following logic: if product A is acceptable to the public and has a risk factor greater than that of product B, everything else equal, the product B is acceptable. The risk-benefit analysis uses the willingness-to-pay criterion such as how much a high risk job pays. This method precludes the need to set a fixed level of acceptable risk since it depends upon the benefits, which vary greatly across products and activities.

      This section has covered the importance of gathering reliable and impartial information for a just and efficient allocation of resources. In the next section we examine the issues of depletable (nonrecyclable and recyclable) resources, the possibilities and probabilities of exhaustion, the disposal of solid wastes, and the durability and obsolescence of products.

THE ECONOMICS OF DEPLETABLE RESOURCES

Depletable resources are those resources that cannot be replenished and will eventually be completely exploited or *depleted*. When they can be replenished, though not completely, they are called *recyclable*. Finally, a resource may be depletable even though it is inherently *replenishable*. The stock of non-renewable resources can be measured as: (1) *current reserves* -- the amount of resources that can be extracted at current prices; (2) *potential reserves* -- the amount that could be extracted if the price was higher; and (3) *resource endowment* -- the total amount of resource on the earth's crust which constitutes the upper limit on the availability of resources. The United States Bureau of Mines keeps records of the U.S. resource base using the classification system according to Table IV.1.

Table IV.I A Taxonomy of Resources

		Total Resources				
		Identified			Undiscovered	
		Demonstrated		Inferred	Hypothetical	Speculative
		Measured	Indicated			
E c o n o m i c		Reserves				
Para-marginal		Subeconomic				
Sub-marginal						

(1) Economic Principles Regarding Depletable Resources in General

When resources cannot be stored their potential reserves are negligible. For example, helium exists in very low concentrations in the atmosphere and as such is too expensive to extract. However, it can be extracted together with natural gas. Consequently, the amount of helium reserves depends upon the amount of natural gas that can be extracted and stored. Other depletable resources are entirely consumed in the production and consumption processes and thus they are not recyclable; e.g. oil, gas, coal. While depletable resources can be exhausted, the rate of depletion can be increased or decreased by economic factors. Higher prices stimulate recycling, the search for substitutes and also encourage technological changes that can increase the availability of depletable resources.

a. Efficient Rates of Depletion -- A concern for society is the potential suddenness of the exhaustion of a depletable resource, without warning. The fear is that the standards of living may fall drastically until new sources or substitutes are found. An efficient rate of depletion would exist if the rate at which a resource is exhausted was equal to the rate that its consumption declined, so that exhaustion and abstinence would occur simultaneously. The efficient criterion was developed in the previous section, i.e., the maximization of net present value of the resource to society. In its most simple form, if marginal extraction costs are zero the rate of extraction should equal the interest rate. This is known as the *Hotelling rule*. When marginal extraction costs are positive the intertemporal maximization approach is applied.

Marginal user cost is defined as the opportunity cost of the future benefits foregone and the *marginal extraction cost* of a resource is assumed to be constant, i.e., that the additional costs of extracting one more unit of a resource is the same regardless of the amount of reserves. As more of the resource is extracted the marginal user cost increases due to the increased scarcity. This allows the producer to raise the price. The higher relative scarcity is reflected in a steady expansion of the marginal user costs even when marginal extraction costs remain constant. The increase in marginal user costs can be appropriated by the owner of the resource through higher prices. In response to these rising costs the quantity extracted falls over time. On the demand side, the higher price lowers consumption until both supply and demand simultaneously equal zero. This occurs because if the supply exceeds the demand, the rate of price increase will decelerate, increasing the use of the resource and its depletion. Alternatively, if the demand exceeds the supply, the higher price will accelerate the lowering of consumption. In this model a resource does not run out "suddenly", though eventually it does run out.

If there are increasing marginal extraction costs -- as in the case of minerals, where ores of lower grades are more costly to extract -- marginal user costs *decline* over time. Remember, marginal user cost is the opportunity cost of future foregone benefits. As it becomes more expensive to extract the resource in the future, the *benefits accruing to future generations diminish.* When the marginal cost of extraction becomes so high, there is a point at which the benefits, the opportunity costs of current extraction, drop to zero. Abstinence has been reached, consumption drops to zero. In this case, the resource is not completely exhausted; some of it is left in the ground because it is too expensive to take out. Again the depletion is smooth; the rate of depletion is constrained by the demand.

The depletion rate of non-renewable resources will be reduced if new sources and substitutes can be found. The marginal cost of extracting a substitute will determine the point at which a switch will be made. As long as the marginal cost of the depletable resource is less than the marginal cost of finding and extracting a substitute, only the depletable resources will be used. The *switch point* occurs when both marginal costs are the same. Similarly, the marginal cost of exploration relative to the marginal cost of extraction will determine when new reserves can be put into place. Technological progress will also tend to lower the rate of depletion because it lowers the marginal costs of extraction, substitution, and exploration. The important point is that under certain economic conditions a *sudden* depletion of a non-renewable resource can be ruled out.

b. Markets and Efficient Allocations -- As long as natural resources are held under a system of private property rights, an efficient allocation is possible. Exclusivity, universality, transferability, and enforceability of rights under a competitive market structure are necessary and sufficient conditions for an efficient allocation of resources. Prices are the signals to conserve scarce natural resources.

c. Market Failures -- As explained in Chapter I, the market does not efficiently allocate society's resources in the presence of externalities. When extraction creates an environmental damage (e.g., strip mining) or begets health hazards (e.g., uranium mining) the marginal social costs are higher that the prices unless costs are internalized.

The model also assumes that the future of benefits foregone are *discounted* at some market interest rate. This discount rate is set by the actions of each individual producer. There is no way to determine if the *social rate of discount* is actually equal to the *private rate.* In the last section we saw that if the private rate is greater than the social rate the resource will be depleted faster than is socially desirable.

It also assumes perfect or sufficient competition, in the sense that if there are no artificial barriers to entry, market prices tend to reflect marginal social costs. It is usually conceded that monopolists restrict output and generate higher prices than those that would prevail under competition. Thus, it can be argued that monopoly tends to lead to resource conservation, though this may depend upon elasticities of demand, a topic to be covered in the next section.

(2) Depletable, Non-recyclable Resources: Oil, Gas, Coal, and Uranium

These resources are among society's most important because they are all sources of energy. In an efficient allocation scheme they are all substitutes and the transition from one to another should be smooth and harmonious. In the event of a total exhaustion of these resources, there are renewable sources that could be tapped, namely fusion or solar energy. The history of the transition from one of these resources to the other has not been smooth -- "energy crises" have not been isolated events. How has the market mechanism handled this problem?

a. Price and Income Elasticities -- We need to understand how consumers respond to changes in some of the relevant variables that affect their decision making. Economics defines *price elasticity* as the *sensitivity* of consumption to changes in prices. If consumers respond significantly the demand is said to be elastic, if the response is not great the demand is inelastic[7].

The price elasticity largely depends upon the availability of substitutes, the opportunities of alternative sources, and the costs relative to total expenditures. Consumers do not respond equally in the short-term as in the long-term. The longer the time to search for substitutes and alternative sources the higher the elasticity. Hence elasticities tend to be higher in the long-term.

The income elasticity of demand is a similar concept. It involves changes in consumption due to changes in income. All other things being equal, the higher the income elasticity the higher the price would have to rise to bring the demand to zero (in the absence of substitutes). The income elasticity is also important because it affects consumption during the business cycles. The higher the response of consumers to income the more business cycle affects consumption. As we shall see later, these elasticities play an important role in the transition from one source of energy to another, particularly with respect to the cartelization of energy sources, conservation efforts, and the effects of government policies.

b. Price Controls -- The oil, gas, and coal sectors cannot be characterized as free or competitive markets. There has been, and there continues to be considerable government intervention, each of which has its own set of economic consequences. Price controls on natural gas began in 1938. The ceiling on gasoline was imposed in 1971 as part of general price controls to reduce inflation. To promote exploration and production of new oil, controls were imposed on "old" domestic oil, thereby providing a standard textbook case for the analysis of price controls.

A price ceiling creates an artificial shortage (see Figure IV.3) because it increases the relative value of the product but lowers the profitability of production. The combined effect distorts the allocation and the transition process. Since it lowers the profitability of the resource: (1) the time of transition from one source of energy to another is shortened; and (2) the transition is abrupt. For example, natural gas price controls motivate users to install natural gas equipment only to discover--after the transition--that it was premature to use the new technology when price controls are lifted.

If expected to be permanent, price ceilings reallocate resources toward the present. If producers expect the lifting of controls in the near future they have the incentive to stop production and wait for the higher prices. The unfortunate effects will be reflected in, what maybe termed, an overshoot and collapse syndrome, caused by government regulation rather than relying on market incentives. The abruptness or suddenness of shifting from one source of energy to another also depends upon the price elasticity of demand. If the demand is inelastic, i.e, if it does not respond very much to changes in prices, then we should not expect a significant switching. The more elastic (sensitive) the larger the adjustment; hence, the longer the price controls, the less manageable the change.

Price controls are usually imposed to avoid *scarcity rents*. Higher prices lead to higher profits and lower consumer surplus. By imposing price controls, the government lowers profitability, therefore, scarcity rent. However, scarcity rent is an opportunity cost that serves the distinct purpose of protecting future consumers. By lowering scarcity rents, price controls transfer resources from future consumers toward present consumers.

c. Cartels -- From the outset of the Industrial Revolution, the world energy needs had been steadily increasing but they had nonetheless been satisfied. Apparently a sense of complacency had developed, until 1973, when the world was shocked by the oil embargo of the Organization of Petroleum of Exporting Countries (OPEC). The oil crisis caused by OPEC also brought awareness that a *cartelization* of countries that are exporters of natural resources could in many ways distort markets and create serious problems throughout the world.

A *cartel* is a *collusive agreement* among producers to increase the price by restricting supply so that in effect the cartel behaves exactly as a monopolistic firm. Cartels violate the perfect competitive conditions by restricting supply and raising prices thereby undermining economically efficient outcomes, as described in Chapter I. In the case of OPEC, the cartel was initiated by member governments in response to what they had believed to be an oligopsony (few buyers of a resource) comprised of the multinational oil companies. A

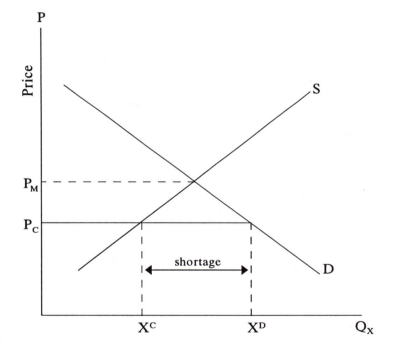

FIGURE IV.3

monopolist can extract higher scarcity rent from a depletable source base because it lowers supply and raises prices.   While it benefits the cartel to delay the transition to a substitute resource, the higher prices of the cartel's product will serve to motivate consumers to conserve and other producers to search for substitutes.

For a cartel, to exist, some stringent conditions are required: very inelastic demand, low income elasticity, internal cohesion (similar cost structures), and enforcement mechanisms.

* A cartel can raise the price easily if the demand is inelastic and consumption is stable. Because the demand for oil is very inelastic in the short-run, OPEC successfully increased the price of oil. The cartel loses market power when alternative sources are found. This is exactly what happened. Although oil substitutes exist, they are expensive and the transition is long. Coal and nuclear energy are clearly alternatives, but both raise serious environmental concerns. The ultimate substitute, solar power, has been used for hot-water heating but remains expensive for many other uses.   Nevertheless, the substitution process that ensued weakened the power of OPEC to set prices.

* A low income elasticity means that the cartel can readily increase the price because consumers do not react to their loss of income. The world economy had been growing and as income grew the demand for energy increased, providing a source of strength to the cartel to increase prices. However, the oil embargo also caused a world recession so that the income elasticity worked against the cartel.

* If the members of the cartel face similar demand and cost structures then it is easier to maintain internal cohesion and consensus. However, if the demand facing an individual member is more elastic than for other members, it benefits the individual member of the cartel to lower its price. It can be shown that, if the demand is elastic, although the lower price reduces revenues, the increase in sales more than overcompensates; as a result, total revenues and profits increase. Lower production costs of some members also beget incentives to cheat by selling at a lower price.

* The tendency for cartel members to cheat requires an enforcement mechanism. At the beginning OPEC required almost none, but the emergence of oil producing countries not affiliated with OPEC has made it almost impossible to enforce the price.

The conditions for a successful cartel existed in 1973 but by 1993 OPEC had lost much of its power, though its presence in the world had a very informative role.

d. The National Security as an Issue -- OPEC brought attention to the possibilities of cartelization in other strategic raw materials. The oil embargo also demonstrated the political power to cajole reluctant adversaries into foreign policy concessions. National security is a classic case of public goods. Since no individual importer finds it convenient to incorporate national security costs in the price (if some do it and the rest do not their profits will be less--a phenomenon known as the *free rider* problem), strategic imports should include costs that are not reflected in the marketplace. These additional costs are called the *vulnerability premium* (Tietenberg, 1992:169).

The vulnerability premium can be reduced by: (1) aggressive diplomacy to avoid embargoes; (2) economic and non-economic restrictions on imports; and (3) domestic incentives to increase domestic production. Examples of (2) and (3) follow.

- Contingency measures such as the *strategic petroleum reserve* can be taken.

- Tariffs and quotas on oil imports will make foreign oil more expensive. Taxes are ways to internalize the public good costs. However, quotas redistribute wealth from consumers to importers. Tariffs and quotas benefit domestic producers.

- Taxes on gasoline and on energy consumption will reduce domestic consumption but will not necessarily reduce the *proportion* of domestic to foreign oil used.

- Subsidies to domestic suppliers (oil or oil substitutes) will motivate domestic production and the search for alternative sources. However, subsidies will not dampen domestic consumption.

None of these measures, by themselves, are completely efficient or socially desirable. However, in the absence of a market mechanism a combination of them may be a second-best solution. Still, the market forces may not be sufficient to correct the imbalances. The public good nature of national security and externalities are sufficient reasons for concern. Nevertheless, the potential for efficient management of energy resources by the political and economic institutions clearly exist.

f. Potential Alternative Sources of Energy -- If the market price for oil is sufficiently high, a transition to other sources may be necessary, but what are these other sources? Are the alternatives socially desirable? Other sources of energy currently available besides coal and nuclear power are:

(i) *Heavy Oil* -- It has been estimated that California and Venezuela have large reserves of heavy oil, amounting to more than the U.S. proven reserves of lighter oil (Howe, 1979:190).

(ii) *Deep Ocean Petroleum* -- It appears very likely that large supplies of gas and oil occur in deep waters beyond the continental shelves; however, no engineering data are available to determine the size of these reserves.

(iii) *Oil Shale* -- Oil shales are fine-grained sedimentary rock containing organic matter capable of yielding oil. Major deposits have been sampled in Colorado, Scotland, Sweden, China, and the former Soviet Union, though no reliable data exist as to how much.

(iv) *Tar Sands* -- There are deposits of consolidated or unconsolidated rocks that contain a very viscous to solid bitumen. However, no technology has been developed yet to convert it to fuel. There are deposits in Utah and Canada.

(v) *Natural Gas* -- Probably the most likely fuel to be used in the future. The growth of this fossil fuel surpasses that of oil and coal and will continue to do so because of new exploration and production techniques. It emits less carbon per unit of energy produced and is likely to benefit from efforts to slow global warming (Flavin, 1992: 46).

(vi) *Gas in Geopressure Zones* -- Some geological formations hold methane--in supersaturated water--that can be exploited with known technologies. Most of them appear to exist in the Gulf of Mexico but the size of reserves is unknown.

(vii) *Gas Hydrates* are frozen natural gas pockets discovered in Russia and Canada. Russian technologists believe very large deposits of such gas exist.

(viii) *High Dry Rock and Geothermal Energy* -- Energy could be tapped from hot rock strata far below the earth's surface and geysers and other geothermal sources could also be utilized.

This information does not cover all potential sources but it suggests that the energy future may not be as pessimistic nor as optimistic as some may think. There are alternative sources but none are without difficulties or complications.

(3) Depletable, Recyclable Resources: Minerals

Economic geologists have frequently pictured the occurrence of minerals as a pyramid with relatively small quantities of high concentration ore at the top and deposits of lower quality at the base. However, this view has been challenged and it has been shown that there are minerals that exhibit sharp boundaries and small variations in concentration while others show a gradual reduction in quality.

The current view is that the economic characteristics of mineral supplies (size, location, average concentration) define three levels divided by two thresholds:

• A potential economic threshold, i.e, the lowest concentration at which extraction is likely to be profitable. Above the economic threshold lies current production and known reserves.

• A mineralogical threshold represents the minimal set of natural conditions that permits the recovering of the mineral among ordinary rocks. Below the mineralogical threshold the element is highly dispersed and its separation from the surrounding rock is currently not possible.

• Between these two thresholds, reserves have been identified but their extraction is currently not economically feasible, however, higher prices and improvements in technology may induce production in the future.

The first threshold is an economic constraint; the average crust abundance threshold is a physical constraint. The economic threshold can be crossed with substantial inputs of energy whose justification requires a considerable increase in the price of the natural resource or significant improvements in technology. Alternatively, the mineralogical constraint can be viewed as a physical impossibility. In this chapter we examine how an efficient market, devoid of imperfections, would deal with the first threshold and how externalities and other factors affect its performance.

a. An Efficient Allocation of Recyclable Resources -- Initially, the virgin ore is exploited because it is cheapest. As more concentrated ores are depleted miners turn to lower grade ores as well as to foreign sources of richer ores. As the costs of extraction increase, the prices of virgin material and finished products also increase. As prices rise, producers may switch from one resource to another, consumers may switch from throwaways to reusable products, and entrepreneurs may adopt new technologies. This model of efficient markets relies on *switch points,* i.e., when the marginal costs of an activity exceed those of an alternative, rational producers and consumers abandon the more expensive in favor of the less expensive one. This switching depends upon the *elasticity of substitution* between resources as well as the *price and income elasticities* of demand. An efficient market would balance the consumption between disposable and recyclable products, between domestic and import sources of mineral ores, and between depletable and renewable raw materials. Nowhere is this process more evident than in recycling.

When land is plentiful waste is inexpensive to dispose of, but as population grows and land becomes scarce, the increasing costs of virgin ores and of disposal makes recycling attractive. Consumers would also find that products relying on virgin ore are more expensive so they would tend to switch to less expensive recyclable products. As long as consumers are made to bear the cost of disposal the use of recyclables tends to increase.

However, recycling is not costless. There are costs associated with collection, separation, transportation, and processing. Only when the costs of extraction increase and the scarcity is reflected by sufficiently high prices of the final products so as to make recycling competitive will there be a switch to recyclable materials and products. When recycling becomes economically attractive manufacturers also design products that facilitate recycling.

What are the market imperfections that distort the switching points? Are the elasticities sufficiently high as to warrant smooth transitions? If the market is not efficient, how could it be corrected?

b. Market Imperfections -- Sometimes the market may be efficient, but other factors such as national security may be important for the allocation of the resources. Other times prices may be too slow to react, or externalities and social risks may be the predominant factors.

(i) *The National Interest Issue* -- As in the case of oil, dependency on foreign sources has an added vulnerability cost. To reduce this risk premium, tariffs, taxes, subsidies, and strategic stockpiling can be established.

(ii) *Elasticities* -- Econometric models and *what if* models have been developed to study the vulnerability of the United States with respect to strategic metals (titanium, vanadium, cobalt, columbium, cadmium, tin-alloys). They show that small disruptions can be safely handled through domestic stockpiles and that the elasticities of substitution are low in the short-term; i.e., changes in prices have small to negligible effects. However, in the long-term prices have considerable effects (Tietenberg, 1992:200).

(iii) *Decisions under Uncertainty* -- Exploration, development, and substitution are not without risks. When risks are included in the costs, switching points are delayed. The decision process involving uncertainty is studied by *Bayesian methodology* which basically establishes an *upper bound* on the value of the additional information needed for a good and an efficient decision. Since all information cannot be acquired or used, only an optimal amount of information will be gathered. However, if this optimal amount or upper boundary is less than the *socially relevant* information then there are external benefits compelling state intervention. Government agencies such as the U.S. Bureau of Mines can provide such information thus internalizing the external benefits.

(iv) *Waste Disposal and Pollution* -- After the products using natural resources are consumed we must dispose of the residuals, as indicated earlier in Figure III.2. Another market imperfection arises from the external costs of disposal. Disposal costs are critical for switching. If individuals do not bear these costs, then the use of virgin ore will be favored over recycling. Littering of highways is a typical example. It is relatively costless to an individual to throw containers out of a car, but it is costly to society. Effluent taxes, refundable deposits, recycling incentive taxes, product disposal charges, have been ways designed to internalize the costs.

The costs of recycling must also be weighted against the costs of disposing the waste in landfills. For some[8], recent technological developments in disposal can make environmentally suitable landfills less expensive than recycling from the point of view of disposal costs. The external costs, like the loss of property values to surrounding areas, can be internalized by proper compensation. Such solutions are more economically attractive than simple prohibition of new landfills.

c. Product Durability -- It is not uncommon to hear that manufacturers implant *planned obsolescence* into their products and that this is a cause for premature resource exhaustion. Durability, which can be designed into a product, also depends very much upon the consumers' choice for it. If consumers value a durable product more than a disposable one, they should be willing to pay more for it and this in turn should induce producers to make more durable products. Such results are expected to occur when there is competition and consumers are well informed.

Products that last longer also cost more. Consumers' decisions to purchase durable goods depend on the present value of the stream of net benefits provided by the product which is in turn determined by the rate of discount, as previously discussed. If individual discount rates are higher than the social rate (the social opportunity cost), consumers would be *undervaluing durability* because the present value of benefits of durable goods is lower than their social value. If individuals use lower rates, they are overvaluing them. A study by Jerry Hausman (1979:33-54) revealed that the lower the income the higher the discount, implying that poor people tend to buy less durable goods. However, the design of policies to correct such undervaluation may have more to do with a reduction in poverty than with the durability of products *per se*. Though market imperfections are not absent from the issues of non-renewable recyclable resources, there are market forces propelling efficient and rational solutions.

(4) Depletable, Replenishable Resources: Water

Water is essential for life, whether it is used to grow food or replace body fluids. The earth's water supply is governed by the hydrologic cycle, a system of continuous water circulation, as described in Chapter II. Only a fraction of the earth's water is available each year for human use. There are two available sources, *surface* and *ground* water. Though both are affected by geographic distribution, weather patterns, pollution, and contamination, most of ground water has been accumulated over geological time and is practically a depletable resource. Surface water appears to be abundant for all humanity, however, this could be misleading because: (1) the geographic distribution of water is uneven; and (2) water flows are stochastic, requiring the estimation of probability distributions of water streams in order to regulate and control its randomness. Apart from the technological aspects of water supply, there are a host of political, social, and economic interests that have turned water policy into one of the most disputed issues in the world.

a. Water Rights and the Efficient Economic Solution -- As previously addressed, an efficient solution depends on well-specified and enforceable private property rights structure to reduce uncertainty and to assure that the benefits and costs of water are reflected in society's calculation. Transferable rights allow the user to face the full cost of water and to reallocate scarce water by selling or leasing it so it can gravitate to its highest-valued use. In the United States, water resources are not held under a system of private property rights.

During the settlement of the Western United States, the right to water belonged to the owner of the adjacent land. *Riparian* rights was an appropriate solution as long as there was enough water for everybody. As land became scarce so did water. Because riparian rights made no provisions for the diversion of water, a change in property rights structures occurred. In California, early gold miners devised a system of "first in time, first in right" for allocating water. Each claimant had a right to divert a specific amount of water from a stream according to this legal principle. Those with more water rights were able to sell the rights to others and water marketing was not unusual. This system prevailed until 1902 when the right to the water was transferred to the state. Since then, the government has *status rights* (see Chapter III) over water and claimants are given *usufructuary* rights rather than an ownership right.

An efficient allocation requires a balance between alternative users. For surface water, an acceptable way to handle the season-to-season variations in water flows is of concerned, while, for ground water, intergenerational considerations must also be included. Since all competing users have a legitimate claim to water the *equimarginal value principle* can be reasonably applied. This principle states that, at the margin, all uses must be equal in relative value or the marginal net benefits to all and each use must be the same. If one use is marginally more valuable than another, water should be diverted to the more valuable use. As the water supply increases for this use, its relative marginal benefits fall, however, in the sector where water became more scarce, the marginal benefits to water increase. An efficient allocation will emerge only when the marginal net benefits to all uses are the same. While transferable rights would ideally allow the diversion of water from less to more valuable uses, there are two difficult problems, one concerns the estimation of net benefits, the other, deciding whose benefits will be considered.

Ground water exhaustibility must also be included in the allocation of water use over time because the resource will be mined until either the supply is depleted or the marginal cost of pumping additional water becomes prohibitive. The case of ground water is exactly like the case of depletable resources. The opportunity cost of the water left in the ground must be weighed against the marginal extraction costs, the present value of using it, and the costs of making surface water available as a substitute to underground supplies.

Instream uses of water, such as fishing, boating, or wildlife habitat, have increased in value over the years. Sport and commercial fishing compete with recreational uses. The value of rivers and lakes as habitats for wildlife must also be taken into consideration. While property rights to instream uses do not exist or are not well-defined, as their values increase and the technology to monitor water uses improves, it is more likely that a system of private property rights will emerge (Anderson and Leal, 1991:105).

b. Sources of Inefficiencies -- There are a considerable number of limitations that have been placed on water that prevents the attainment of an economic efficient solution. Among the most prevalent are the restrictions to transfers, nonmarket pricing, and exclusion of demand factors in the determination of supply (such as rapid population growth or flat rates).

(i) *Legal Restrictions to Transfers* -- A major stumbling block to water marketing is the legal precedent for postulating a relationship between diversion and *beneficial use*. Users must put their water to beneficial use or lose their rights to it. The courts have established diversion as a prerequisite to beneficial use thus basically denying the option of private appropriation and transferability.

A second restriction is that of *preferential* use. The government sets the ranking for water use. Though water scarcities fluctuate over time and across geographic regions, this system locks-in preferential use for agriculture regardless of the relative values of other uses. Even when urban and other users are willing and able to pay to acquire water, the government impedes the diversion away from agricultural uses.

(ii) *Water Pricing* -- Price regulators usually adopt a rate structure that includes a price for water that does not fully reflect the marginal costs of providing water services. In some cases, consumers pay a flat rate for water. Such a system leads to wasteful water consumption and too little conservation. A solution to this problem is increasing block rates. Under this system the higher the use of water, the higher the price.

(iii) *Subsidies and Federal Reclamation Projects* -- Reclamation projects subsidized by the government also distort the relative valuation between alternative water uses. The costs of expanding the water supply for rapidly increasing populations have been met by public investment and subsidies, state and federal taxpayers end up providing the revenues that should be borne by new residents. Several of the Bureau of Reclamation's water projects have been built as a result of congressional political actions rather than being based on economic or national interest decisions (Howe, 1986). The need of approval by government agencies for water allocation increases uncertainty and provides room for inefficient political practices.

c. Some Potential Remedies -- The transferability of water for different uses is desirable, though it is often difficult to implement. Nevertheless, once the government makes its initial assignment of rights to the parties of interest, some gains in efficiency can be obtained by allowing the selling of water. Those who value water more than others should be willing and able to pay for it. For example, in England and Scotland, private angling associations purchase fishing rights from landowners which in turn sell them to their members (Anderson and Leal, 1991:112). In addition, such rights can be granted to or acquired by environmental or Non-Government Organizations (NGOs) for the protection of wildlife habitats.

Marginal costs of water supplies should be included in water rates. As previously mentioned, increasing rates will encourage conservation and more efficient uses. If water meters with clocks are installed, water rates could be increased during peak demands. Expansion of water supplies should be prorated, so that newcomers would pay more than current residents. This would mitigate the pressure placed by rapid immigration to some cities where water is scarce, like Tucson, Arizona.

If policy makers are interested in garnering the rewards of market efficiencies, they must find ways to define property rights in water, enforce them, and make them transferable, and then guard them against doctrines that erode these principles. In the following section we will analyze the market and non-market forces that affect the supply and perishability of renewable resources, specially timber and fish.

THE ECONOMICS OF RENEWABLE RESOURCES

Forests and fisheries are *renewable* but *destructible* resources, but markets and economic principles can be used to understand how efficient solutions can be achieved. These same principles can highlight the roots of inefficiencies so that appropriate policies for correcting them can be identified. Forestry -- whether for timber or for recreational uses, as a habitat for rare species, as wildlife sanctuaries, or as protection for watersheds -- is a vital natural resource. Forest land management was probably the earliest example of the formal application of economic principles to the management of natural resources. Fisheries are an important resource for food and recreational purposes. One of the problems associated with the efficient management of fisheries concerns the assignment of property rights. As we have seen, this is a challenge to the application of market solutions.

(1) Storable Renewable Resources: Forests

According to the most recent United Nations data, world forest land today covers 4 billion hectares, more than 30 percent of the total global land area. According to the U.S. Forest Service, 22 million new cubic feet of wood are grown in the United States with a net annual growth of 27 percent in commercial harvesting. Throughout New England the amount of land covered by forests has been steadily increasing, following the loss of 136 million hectares between 1630 and 1920 (Brown, 1992:95). According to Jerry Taylor (1993:375), the real prices of lumber and paper have fallen by 10 to 25 percent since 1980. When indexed by wages, lumber prices in 1980 were one-third of those in 1950, one-sixth of those in 1900, and one-tenth of those in 1800.

Trees take a long time to mature. An efficient use and exploitation of the resource requires: (1) how best to accommodate the multiple uses of forest lands; (2) careful management to maximize the fertility of the land; (3) when and how to harvest timber from the lands that are sufficiently productive to warrant harvesting; and (4) when and how to replant in order to achieve an optimum rotation.

In economics, trees resemble the production and use of *capital goods*. Capital goods are the physical goods--machinery, equipment, factory plants, tools--used to produce other goods. Unlike capital goods, however, timber is subject to many externalities.

a. The Biological Dimension -- Initially, when trees are very young, growth is rather slow in volume. A period of rapid volume growth follows until the tree slows its growth, stops or even reverses. The actual growth of a tree depends upon many physical factors such as weather, soil fertility, cultivation practices, forest fires, and air pollution.

A tree, according to foresters, should be harvested at an age when its size--known as the *mean annual increment* (MAI)--has reached a maximum; that is when the tree has reached the largest volume relative to age. This biological rule is calculated by dividing the cumulative volume of a stand at the end of each decade by the cumulative number of years the stand has been growing up to that decade. From the economic point of view this rule is arbitrary. It does not reflect the value of the timber, the money invested in the forest, or the costs of planting and/or harvesting--all important considerations for efficient management.

b. Efficient Economic Decisions -- When an area is considered for timber growing, decisions must be made as to what age the trees should be harvested, when the area will be replanted (or allowed to grow again from natural reseeding), and how big the trees should be allowed to grow or up to what age, etc. The optimal harvesting time depends upon: (1) the costs of planting; (2) the price of cut timber; (3) the rate of discount applicable to future costs and receipts; and (4) the pattern of growth of useful timber associated with the age and the volume of the tree. There are two facets of opportunity costs involved in this process: (1) the financial capital invested in trees; and (2) the land occupied by the trees that could be employed for alternative income producing activities.

From our definition of efficiency, the optimal rotation would be the time that maximizes the present value of the net benefits from the wood. When markets are efficient, the market value of a newly cut or newly planted piece of land would have to be at least equal to the best alternative foregone for which the land could have been used. The discounted value of the anticipated stream of benefits minus expenditures when the land is kept in timber production is called *the site expectation value*. Before analyzing optimal harvesting times, it should be noted that some of the costs that are relevant for the multiple rotation case need not be considered in the single rotation case.

(i) *A single rotation case* -- The optimal harvesting time occurs when the marginal benefit of an additional year's growth is equal to the opportunity cost of capital. When the capital gains from letting the trees grow one more year become equal to the return that can be obtained from harvesting the trees and investing the gains, the trees will be harvested. Harvesting times depend upon the discount rates, the higher the discount rate the shorter the harvesting time.

The magnitude of the planting and harvesting costs do not affect the optimal rotation time in the single period case, while they do affect the efficient outcome in the multiple period case. Planting costs are *sunk costs* to the extent that they are constant and belong to the past, which is unchangeable. Once the decision to plant is carried out, sunk costs cannot be recovered if future profits turn out to be negative. Planting costs, however, do affect the decision in the planning stage. In fact, if they were expected to exceed the value of benefits, no planting would ever take place. Harvesting costs are proportional to the amount of wood harvested and they rise or fall as the volume of timber to be harvested increases or falls. Hence, they do not affect rotation time either. Similarly, taxes have no effect on the optimal time because they change the net benefit value, thus lowering the fertility curve but without changing the location of the optimum point.

(ii) *Multiple rotation case* -- If multiple periods are considered, there are interdependencies between the periods. The harvesting decision must reflect such interdependencies. In an infinite planning horizon, the opportunity cost of delaying the next cycle must be covered by the gain in tree growth as well as other costs considered in the single period model. The optimal rotation time is shorter in the infinite-planning case than in the single-period case because the marginal cost of a delay is higher due to the existence of the opportunity cost of starting the cycle later.

Planting costs in this case do matter; higher planting costs reduce the marginal opportunity cost of delaying the cycle, and as a result, rotation time increases.   A similar result is obtained if harvesting costs increase.   The imposition of taxes also lengthens the harvesting time. Furthermore, lengthening the rotation time implies that the older trees will be harvested resulting in higher volumes of wood.

Timber prices also play a role in determining harvesting time in the multi-period model.   Rising prices offset the effect of discounting since higher prices can cover the opportunity costs of not harvesting.   In essence, rising prices imply longer rotation periods.   Other considerations, such as fires, habitats for wildlife, recreational opportunities, and the stabilization of watersheds represent externalities that must be incorporated in the model. The internalization of these factors should delay harvesting because the effect of additional benefits is similar to that of higher prices.

An ideal model in forestry is that of the *fully regulated* forest.   It implies a series of forest plots, each with trees of different ages.   A sufficient number of plots would be available to provide trees of every age up to the age at which they are harvested.   At the optimal rotation time the wood is harvested and the plot is restocked.   In this way, harvesting can occur without endangering the sustainability of the forest.   There is no economic rationale for a fully regulated forest.   Adopting a policy that gradually transforms the unregulated forest into the fully regulated one can be quite costly in terms of interest on the large inventory and in terms of foregone rapid growth of new plantings.   For example, a rapid cutting of the forest might glut the market, greatly reducing the value of the timber to the disadvantage of the producers. Alternatively, if the volumes involved are relatively small, cutting more rapidly would be to their advantage.

c. Sources of Inefficiency -- Timber and lumber prices are notoriously unstable, especially lumber for residential construction.   Higher uncertainty implies higher risks and consequently shorter rotation times.   Incorrect price expectations can also lead to wrong harvesting-times decisions.   To some extent, price uncertainties and fluctuations can be solved by sales contracts that set the price in the future.   Futures markets allow speculators to purchase the rights to resources and hold them off the market for resale at higher prices in the future.   Futures markets transfer the risk from the producers to speculators.   Whenever prices increase, harvesting is delayed.   In the face of substantial price fluctuations or unanticipated increase in price, the public often reacts by clamoring for government intervention, to increase either wood production and/or to prohibit exports.

It has been shown that the size or the scale of operation is an important factor for efficient market allocations[9].   In addition, efficient operations require investment in large and expensive equipment, sophisticated pest control, access to credit and markets, investment in new technologies, and greater variety of tree species. All of this may tend to generate oligopolistic market structures.

Additional inefficiencies result from air pollution, acid rain, pests, and forest fires -- all externalities imposed upon the foresters with long term effects. The existence of these externalities lowers the incentives to invest in forests. There are also positive and negative externalities imposed by the foresters upon wildlife habitats, recreation, and watersheds. When these benefits or costs are not included, forests will not be managed efficiently.

(2) Renewable Common-Property Resources: Fisheries

As previously developed in Chapter I, the absence of well-defined, well-enforced, and transferable property rights gives rise to congestion, overuse, or excessive exploitation of a resource because the negative externalities are not taken into account by the decision maker. Before we examine the issues of communal property vis-à-vis private ownership, we introduce the differences between a maximum biological yield and an economically efficient yield.

a. Basic Biological Relationships -- In a typical fishery, size is a function of age. As the age of the fish increases so does its size, but at some point growth stops. A year-class (fish spawning the same year) achieves a *maximum biomass* at some age depending upon its physiology and the number of predators it encounters.

Population (stock) size can be described by a yield curve exhibiting a maximum rate of growth G_m and two points of zero growth: G_0 and G_1 (see Figure IV.4). At G_1, the population has attained its carrying capacity resulting in a growth rate of zero. At G_0, the *minimum viable population*, growth is unstable. If some factors shift the population from G_0, it either increases to G_1 or becomes extinct. At G_m the population has reached a size such that a maximum catch can be sustained indefinitely without reducing the size of the population. Biologists call this *the maximum sustainable yield*. It must be emphasized that any yield point above the zero line is sustainable, that is, the catch can be perpetually sustained. If the system is left alone, natural forces will move the rate of growth to G_1, the stable zero rate of growth corresponding to the largest stock of fish.

b. Sustainable Economic Yields: Static and Dynamic -- In static economic terms, a sustainable yield is efficient when the catch level maximizes net benefits while maintaining a constant stock of fish. Such an equilibrium position depends upon: (1) the price of the fish; (2) the marginal cost of a unit of fishing effort; and (3) the distribution curve of growth rates of the fish population. A mirror

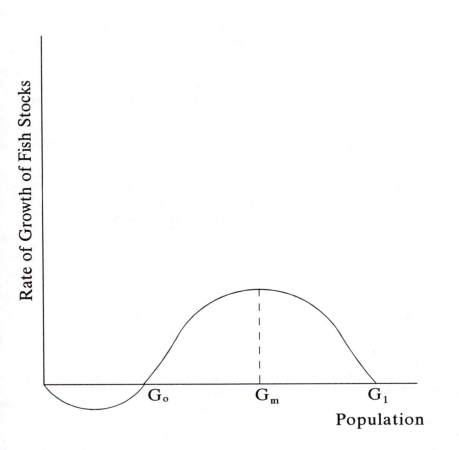

FIGURE IV.4

image of Figure IV.4 can be used to represent the value of benefits from fishing. This benefit curve is intended to reflect the revenues obtained from selling the fish (see Figure IV.5). In Panel b, we reproduce Figure IV.4, slightly modified. Instead of fish stock on the horizontal axis, we now measure fishing effort (e.g. hours of fishing), the rate of growth of fish (yield) is depicted on the vertical axis. For each yield there is a corresponding fishing effort. It must be noted that, after the maximum yield (E_m) is reached, the additional fishing effort lowers the yield. This simply means that the more time that is spent in fishing, the lower the rate of growth of the population of fish. However, the stock will not be depleted even if the fishing effort is so large as to reach point E_1. Only when fishing efforts exceed E_1 will the stock decline.

In Panel a of Figure IV.5, the vertical axis, instead of growth rates, measures the benefits of fishing. The higher the growth rate of the fish, the higher the catch, consequently, the higher the benefits of fishing. There is a maximum level of benefits that can be obtained from a certain fishing effort. This maximum corresponds to the maximum rate of growth at E_m. Since the growth rate of fish diminishes after the maximum yield is attained so do the benefits. But the fishing effort also depends upon the costs. When the marginal costs of fishing are constant, total costs (line TC in the figure) rise. The largest difference between benefits and costs (net benefits or profits) is found when the slopes of the benefits curve and the cost line are equal, that is, where marginal benefits equal marginal costs. This optimum economic point (point E_0 in Panels a and b) occurs at a lower sustainable yield than that determined by biological criteria (E_m).

This static analysis allows us to examine the effects of changes in some of the variables. If the price of fish increases the benefits curve would shift upward; fishing efforts would increase, but the efficiency, relative to the biological maximum, would be lowered. Technological progress can be depicted as a lower-sloped cost line (to the extent that it reduces the marginal costs of efforts). Technology, hence, leads to more fishing and consequently to an efficient sustainable yield lower than before (see Panel a in Figure IV.5). Only when the costs are zero would the economic efficiency criterion coincide with the biologists' highest sustainable growth.

In dynamic terms, the optimal economic yield is again one that maximizes the present value of net benefits of fishing. The dynamic factor introduces an additional cost--the opportunity cost of foregoing current income--which is captured in the discount rate. The increase in costs lowers the effort but raises the efficient sustainable yield. The higher the discount rate the higher the sustainable equilibrium point.

c. The Commons Revisited -- The fisheries in international waters have received much attention because they are typical of the negative externalities

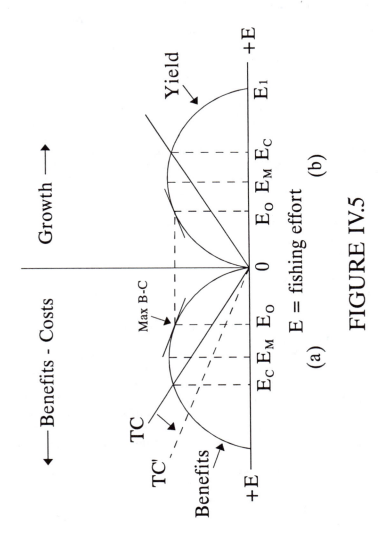

FIGURE IV.5

associated with common property resources (Editor, 1994:21-24). In addition to the concern of permanent destruction, there is also the problem of the distribution of the benefits: who should it have access to the fisheries?

The above economic analysis (part b) illustrates the nature of decision making when the resource owner can exclude others from harvesting the fish. The principle of profit maximization implies the exclusion of others. When the property is a commons, such exclusion is not possible. As each fisherman attempts to exploit the resource before the other one does, competition drives profits to zero (At Point E_c in Panel a Figure IV.5, benefits equal costs). In this case, the fishing effort (Point E_c in Panel b) will correspond to a yield different than the optimal economic (E_0) and biological one (E_m). This *contemporaneous* externality is the reason for overexploitation of the resource. If the size of the stock is reduced, future net benefits are also lowered causing an *intergenerational* externality.

d. The 200-mile-limit to Territorial Waters or How to Appropriate the Commons -- Since most of the profitable fisheries are in the oceans, it matters how such common property should be distributed. In order to deal with this problem nations of the world are continuously negotiating bilaterally and multilaterally through international organizations. A result of such negotiations was the extension of territorial waters to within a 200 mile limit from shore. Within these waters the governments have exclusive jurisdiction to grant fishing permits, grants, concessions, or any other method they may find feasible to implement effective management policies.

One of the international issues constantly being addressed is enforcement policies. In spite of international treaties, lack of enforcement nullifies the exclusion needed for an economically efficient solution. With lax enforcement regulations may be ignored. Furthermore, enforcement efforts are not costless either. Such costs should be included in an efficient solution. When enforcement costs are included, the marginal costs increase. This would result in a smaller population size than would occur when enforcement costs are ignored.

e. Market Solutions -- The common property problem can be alleviated by designing ways to make the market work. There are a variety of market mechanisms for efficient management of resources. Among the feasible market solutions are the leasing or auctioning of public property, such as oyster beds, or tradeable permits as done in Zimbabwe with the elephants.

(i) *Aquaculture*. Raising fish on farms is not new. Indians along the Columbia River developed effective technologies to catch salmon. Shrimp farming is fast becoming a non-traditional source of export revenues. Oyster beds in Louisiana are a classical case study in the use of market forces.

(ii) *Quotas* -- A new approach called *individual tradeable quotas* or ITQs entitles an individual to catch a specified percentage of the total allowable catch. Quota holders face a greater degree of certainty that their share of the catch will not be taken by someone else and transferability allows quotas to end up in the hands of the most efficient fishermen. ITQs encourage reduction in costs because those who implement cost-reducing methods can purchase quotas from the less efficient.

f. Alternative Solutions -- Instead of relying on private property rights, governments have traditionally imposed *status-rights* type regulation for controlling the over-exploitation of resources. On the whole, regulatory schemes focus on the biological maximum sustainable yield and attempt to reach it by increasing the costs of fishing. Regulations, though needed to avoid depletion of resources, if not properly designed to meet procedural requirements and mandates will not result in efficient solutions. For example, if traps are forbidden, fishermen use nets. If nets are forbidden substitute methods are introduced. If regulation becomes overbearing in one area or if regulations are applied only in certain areas and not in others, fishermen move to other regions. In addition, relying on status rights often amounts to a *corset* solution, that is, the problem simply moves somewhere else.

When the number of fishermen are restricted or the season is shortened, fishermen use bigger boats, sonar, and more efficient nets. This leads to overcapitalization, where some groups (deep pocket fishermen) are favored over others. Finally, society's scarce resources are used to both promote regulation and, at the same time, to prevent regulation. These inefficiencies are socially harmful. The structure of property rights provides economic incentives in channeling the allocation of resources whether in fisheries or timber.

ENDNOTES

1. The "total" value of a variable is the area under a "marginal" curve. In our case, a demand curve represents the marginal benefits that a consumer expects to obtain from consuming a good. Therefore, the area under the demand constitutes the value of total benefits. Similarly, the total cost is the price times the quantity consumed (p x q); i.e., the area under the marginal cost (price = MC under perfect competition) represents the total cost. Hence, the difference between the two--depicted by the shaded areas in the figure--is the net benefits obtained by the consumer.

2. A rigorous mathematical derivation can be found in Anthony Fisher (1981).

3. A rational individual maximizes utility when the last unit of each and every good consumed renders the same marginal benefit. Mathematically this is expressed as:

$$\frac{MU_1}{P_1} = \frac{MU_2}{P_2} = \cdots = \frac{MU_n}{P_n}$$

where MU_j is the Marginal Utility of the jth good or service.

4. An intergenerational equity principle has been proposed by Rawls (1971) called the *sustainability criterion* that says: *at a minimum, future generations should be left no worse off than current generations.* Allocations that enrich present generations *at the expense* of future generations *are fair* if future generations do not become worse off or remain the same.

5. These and other examples are presented in Jay Lehr (1992).

6. See for example, Sheldon Krimsky and Dominic Golding (1991: 92-119).

7. All economics textbooks dedicate a good portion of demand theory to elasticities.

8. Clark Wiseman (1992) and George Reisman (1992) argue this point in Lehr (1992).

9. An analysis by Marion Clawson (1975) shows that it does not pay for small holders of land to invest time or money in efficient forest management.

REFERENCES

Anderson, T.L. and Leal, D.R. 1991. *Free Market Environmentalism.* San Francisco: Pacific Research Institute for Public Policy.

Bendfeldt, J.F. 1992. Environmentalism in Latin America: Prospects for an Economy of Natural Resources. In *Free Market Environmentalism.* Fairfax, Virginia: Atlas Economic Research Foundation. May: 5-26.

Brown, Lester. 1992. Forest Shrinking at Record Rate. In *Vital Signs 1992*, eds. Brown, L.R., Flavin, C. and Kane, H. New York: W.W. Norton & Company: 94-95.

Chechile, R.A. 1991. Probability, Utility, and Decision Trees in Environmental Decision Analysis. In *Environmental Decision Making: A Multidisciplinary Approach*, eds. R.A. Chechile and S. Carlisle. New York: Van Nostrand Reinhold: 64-91.

Clawson, M. 1975. *Forests for Whom and For What?.* Washington D.C.: Resources for the Future, Inc.

Dickie, M., Fisher, A. and Gerking, S. 1987. Market Transactions and Hypothetical Demand Data: A Comparative Study. *Journal of the American Statistical Association.* 82 (397): 69-75.

Dietz, F.J. and van der Straaten, J. 1992. Rethinking Environmental Economics: Missing Links between Economic Theory and Environmental Policy. *Journal of Economic Issues* 26 (March): 27-51.

Editor. 1994. The Tragedy of the Oceans. *The Economist* (March 19th): 21-24.

Fisher, A.C. 1981. *Resource and Environmental Economics.* Cambridge Survey of Economic Literature. Cambridge: Cambridge University Press.

Flavin, C. 1992. Natural Gas Production Climbs. In *Vital Signs 1992* eds. L.R. Brown, C. Flavin, H. Kane. New York: W.W. Norton & Company: 46-47.

Freeman III, A.M. 1979. Hedonic Prices, Property Values and Measuring Environmental Benefits: A Survey of the Issues. *Scandinavian Journal of Economics* 81 (2): 154-173.

Hausman, J. 1979. Individual Discount Rates and the Purchase and Utilization of Energy-Using Durables. *Bell Journal of Economics*, 10 (Spring): 33-54

Howe, C.W. 1986. Project Benefits and Costs from National and Regional Viewpoints: Methodological Issues and Case Study of the Colorado-Big Thompson Project. *Natural Resources Journal*, 26 (Winter):

Howe, C.W. 1979. *Natural Resource Economics*. New York: John Wiley & Sons, Inc.

Krimsky, S. and D. Golding. 1991. Factoring Risk into Environmental Decision Making. In *Environmental Decision Making: A Multidisciplinary Approach*, eds. R.A. Chechile and S. Carlisle. New York: Van Nostrand Reinhold: 92-119.

Lehr. J. 1992. A New Measure of Risk. In *Rational Readings on Environmental Concerns*, ed. J. Lehr. New York: Van Nostrand Reinhold: 684-690.

McMillan, M.L. 1979. Estimates of Households' Preferences for Environmental Quality and Other Housing Characteristics from a System of Demand Equations. *Scandinavian Journal of Economics*, 81 (2): 174-187.

Mitchell, R.C. and Carson, R.T. 1992. *Using Survey to Value Public Goods: The Contingent Valuation Method*. Washington D.C.: Resources for the Future, Inc.

Passell, P. 1993. Polls May Help Government Decide the Worth of Nature. *The New York Times* (September 6): 1.

Rawls, J. 1971. *A Theory of Justice*. Cambridge, Massachusetts: Harvard University Press.

Reisman, G.G. 1992. The Growing Abundance of Natural Resources and the Wastefulness of Recycling. In *Rational Readings on Environmental Concerns*, ed. J. Lehr. New York: Van Nostrand Reinhold: 631-636.

Taylor, J. 1993. The Growing Abundance of Natural Resources. In *Market Liberalism*, eds. D. Boaz and E.H. Crane. Washington, D.C.: The Cato Institute: 363-378.

Tietenberg, T. 1992. *Environmental and Natural Resource Economics*. New York: Harper Collins Publishers.

Tregarthen, S. 1990. At What Value Your Life? Economists Estimate the Value of Life. *The Margin* 6 (November/December): 38-39.

Whittington, Dale, Lauria, D.T., Wright, A.M., Choe, K., Hughes, J.A., and Swarna, V. 1993. Household Demand for Improved Sanitation Services in Kumasi, Ghana: A Contingent Valuation Study. *Water Resources Research* 29 (June): 1539-1560.

Williams, J.R. 1992.   The Religion of Environmentalism.   In *Free Market Environmentalism*. Fairfax, Virginia: Atlas Economic Research Foundation: 3-7.

Wiseman, C. 1992. Dumping: Less Wasteful than Recycling.   In *Rational Readings on Environmental Concerns*, ed. J. Lehr. New York: Van Nostrand Reinhold: 637-639.

CHAPTER V

ENVIRONMENTAL ECONOMIC
REMEDIES

EXAMPLE FOR CHAPTER V

The upstream chemical firm and the downstream farmer.

The simple example presented here will be used as the vehicle of analysis for undertaking a review of the several environmental economic remedies that follow. Several simplifying assumptions will be made as we proceed through the review.

A chemical firm, producing a very useful product -- good Y -- is situated along a river upstream from, and adjacent to, a downstream farmer producing -- good X. The chemical firm has well-defined resource markets from which it acquires all of the necessary factors of production needed to produce Y. Due in part to the technology it presently employs, the firm dumps water-borne effluents into the river at several point sources.

The downstream farmer (who also has well-defined resource markets from which he acquires all of the necessary factors of production needed to produce crop X) extracts water from the river through a pumping system and irrigates his crops with the river water. It is initially assumed that the government (perhaps the federal, state, or the local democratic government -- hereafter the "government") has determined that the river is held as a common property resource. It is assumed that there are no other upstream sources of the effluent and that the effluent, for all intents and purposes, dissipates approximately a mile downstream from the farmer's property (see Figure V.1).

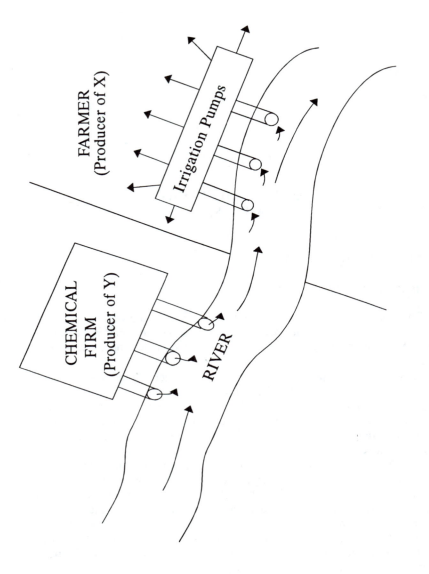

FIGURE V.1

WHY ENVIRONMENTAL PROBLEMS ARISE

It is important to recognize that in most western societies, environmental problems arise for several reasons. Some of these include: (a) the rights to the environmental media are held as a common property resource and the supply of the particular resource does not exceed demand at a zero price, (b) the government has jurisdiction over the rights to the environmental media, and either (i) does nothing about the environmental pollution, or (ii) does not enforce whatever regulations it has set forth to protect the ecological integrity of the environment. In addition, whether the government does or does not pass a regulation to protect the environment (i.e., i or ii above), some environmental problems still arise due to (c) the unintentional acts of producers and/or consumers as well as (d) the intentional acts of some individuals, the latter especially relevant when producers or consumers can anticipate lax enforcement of environmental laws by the government.

It must also be kept in mind that environmental problems (as opposed to natural resource problems) not only come about as a result of the depositing of residuals from economic production (egs., air and water pollution) and economic consumption (egs., driving a car, litter, and noise pollution), but also are due to the secondary environmental effects of resource extraction. Several examples of this latter point include (a) the visual environmental problems associated with offshore oil rigs (a natural resource extraction activity); (b) the despoliation of the environment as a result of strip mining coal (a natural resource extraction activity); (c) the problems associated with subsidence as related to the mining of minerals beneath the earth's surface (the mining, a natural resource activity); (d) the consequent environmental effects of clear cutting forests (a natural resource extraction activity) and (e) the killing of dolphins (and sea turtles) in the process of catching tuna (and shrimp) in nets (with the tuna and shrimp the extracted natural resources).

OPPORTUNITY COSTS OF POLLUTION ABATEMENT

The costs associated with abating the effects of pollution are not one dimensional and costs must be understood from society's standpoint in order to assess the allocative efficiency of various approaches presented here (Seneca and Taussig, 1984:10-17). The economic costs include the sum of the prevention or abatement costs, the clean-up costs, and the welfare damage costs.

The concept of economic efficiency implies that if one were going to undertake a particular course of action -- for example, to pursue a specific environmental initiative to maintain or enhance the environment -- it makes economic sense to accomplish that action at least cost to society. Hence, especially within environmental economics, three different costs have been identified that are relevant to assessing the economic rationale of moving forward with any one of the several remedies that might be available to undertake the specific environmental initiative. Implicit here is the idea that there is never only one way to accomplish a particular environmental initiative. If there is only one option and society has chosen to move forward with that environmental initiative, then it becomes an engineering question, not an economic question. But where there are several options, the concept of efficiency may have a role to play in fashioning remedies.

Throughout this chapter we are operating under the assumption that all cost estimates can be made accurately; the logic of economics entails adopting that remedy which is cost minimizing. From society's standpoint, there are three costs to consider. The three costs include (1) the costs of prevention (CP) -- those costs that would necessarily be incurred to prevent the environmental damage before it occurs; (2) the clean-up costs (CUC) -- those costs that would have to be incurred to clean up and restore the environment after the environmental pollution took place; and (3) the welfare damage costs (WDC) -- the costs associated with living with the negative, external costs imposed upon society due to the environmental damage.

Hypothetically, many possibilities exist; we consider six here. Examples i, ii, and iii assume that no matter which remedy is selected, only one of the three costs will be incurred.

     i. If CP < CUC and CP < WDC, then it makes economic sense to undertake those expenditures necessary to prevent the pollution before it occurs.

     ii. If CUC < CP and CUC < WDC, this implies that by the very nature of this polluting activity, it is quite easy to clean up. Thus, the correct economic strategy is to allow the pollution to occur and then undertake those expenditures that will restore the environment back to its original condition.

     iii. If WDC < CP and WDC < CUC, this implies that the damage society is incurring is simply too insignificant to either prevent the pollution before hand or clean it up afterward. Live with the welfare damage costs.

Examples iv, v, and vi recognize that typically, environmental policies can be constructed so as to have a mix of "prevention," "clean-up," and "live with" remedies -- that is, a mixed policy that incurs some of each cost to implement the environmental initiative. When this is the case, then the logic is quite straight forward.

     iv. Let us assume that a given environmental initiative to reduce the quantity of sulphur dioxide pollution in a region by 20% results in welfare damage costs going from $300 down to $20 yielding $280 in benefits of abatement. Let us further assume that there are three different remedies to accomplish this initiative which look like the following ($):

		B/C Ratio	$Total Costs
Remedy 1-> WDC(20):	CP(80) + CUC(12) =	280/92 = 3.04 *	$112
Remedy 2-> WDC(20):	CP(60) + CUC(35) =	280/95 = 2.95	$115
Remedy 3-> WDC(20):	CP(40) + CUC(70) =	280/110= 2.55	$130

It is clear the society should adopt Remedy 1 which sets the environmental initiative in place by incurring direct costs of $92 ($80 in prevention costs plus $12 in clean up costs) together with $20 in welfare damage costs, in total yielding a minimum societal cost of $112, below the respective costs of the other two options.

v. Alternatively, the government may decide to appropriate so much money to abate sulphur dioxide pollution in a region which is presently causing $300 in WDC. Let us assume it has budgeted $100 for this purpose. Again assume that there are three different remedies each of which will cost $100 in direct expenses (prevention costs plus clean up costs) but yield a different pattern of residual welfare damage costs. The possibilities might look like the following ($):

		B/C Ratio	$Total Costs
Remedy 1-> WDC(35):	CP(80) + CUC(20) =	265/100 = 2.65	$135
Remedy 2-> WDC(30):	CP(55) + CUC(45) =	270/100 = 2.70	$130
Remedy 3-> WDC(25):	CP(30) + CUC(70) =	275/100 = 2.75 *	$125

It is clear the society should adopt Remedy 3 which sets the environmental initiative in place for $100 in direct costs (prevention costs plus clean up costs) and obtains the maximum reduction in WDC $275 (from $300 down to $25). This is done by incurring $30 in prevention costs and $70 in clean up costs together with a welfare damage cost of $25 for a minimum societal cost of $125, below the respective costs of the other two options.

vi. Finally, let us assume that there exists only three different technologies that can be implemented to reduce sulphur dioxide pollution which before any action is undertaken is resulting in WDC equal to $300. Each technology requires its own mix of direct costs and each has a different impact on the welfare damage costs. Consequently, the choice of technology will affect both the stream of benefits (B) as well as the pattern of costs (C):

		B/C Ratio	$Total Costs
Technology 1->WDC(60):	CP(49) + CUC(64) =	240/113 = 2.12	$173
Technology 2->WDC(50):	CP(56) + CUC(58) =	250/114 = 2.19*	$164
Technology 3->WDC(45):	CP(75) + CUC(56) =	255/131 = 1.94	$176

In this case, it is clear that technology 2 should be adopted as it is the technology that provides the greatest net benefits to society. With its adoption, direct costs come to $114 (prevention costs plus clean up costs) and, together with a residual welfare damage costs equal to $50, total costs come to $164. On the other hand, the benefits come to $300 minus $50 which equals $250, the net benefits of pollution abatement. Thus, technology 2 yields the greatest benefit/cost ratio of 2.19. Note that the logic of economics suggests that, sometimes the adoption of the most advantageous benefit-cost solution (technology 2) may mean adopting an environmental remedy that neither (i) minimizes the welfare damage costs to society ($45 as in technology 3) nor (ii) is undertaken at least direct cost to society ($113 as in technology 1).

ENVIRONMENTAL ECONOMICS: OVERVIEW OF THE CONVENTIONAL REMEDIES

(1) Common Property Remedy

As long as the effluent being deposited into the river by the chemical firm has no appreciable effect on the farmer's crops, then, based on the economic efficiency criteria, the chemical firm should be allowed to continue to use the river in the manner as so indicated. That is, since the demand for the irrigation use of the river's water does not exceed its supply at a zero price, it makes economic sense to maintain the river as a common property resource. As has been established by Garrett Hardin, in the event demand should exceed supply at a zero price, "freedom in the commons brings ruin to all." (Hardin, 1968; see also Ostrom, 1990).

(2) The Coase Solution[1] -- Zero Transactions Costs

Under the present case, it was assumed that the farmer was earning a rate of return sufficient to keep the farm land from being used in any alternative use and to keep the farmer from changing his occupation. Now, let us additionally assume that the effluent of the chemical firm does in fact degrade the water quality resulting in significant crop damage by lessening the productivity of the downstream farmer (a form of external costs XC where MCp is now less than MCs -- in terms of equation #4 in Chapter I, given XC, MCp < MCs). Clearly, in this case, society economically gains by the additional amount of chemical production, but at the same time incurs a loss due to the crop damage brought on by the water pollution.

As demonstrated by Ronald H. Coase, as long as the transactions costs are zero, a market solution could be called upon to find the most economically efficient solution to this problem, i.e., the optimal amount of pollution abatement that results in the allocatively efficient amount of chemical production (Y) and crop production (X). This remedy (under the zero transactions costs assumption) requires that the government do one of two things. Once having recognized the problem, the government must act to make the chemical firm liable for the damages its actions caused to the farmer's crops, that is, *give the rights to the farmer*; or, alternatively, the government must *give the rights to the chemical firm* by not making the firm liable for the damages caused to the farmer. It should be clear, but nonetheless worth reiterating here, that the proposed Coase solutions in this and the subsequent two sections of this chapter (3. Coase Solution - Positive Transactions Costs, and 4. The Conglomerate Firm), represent possible remedies that rely on the market sector as opposed to alternative remedies that rely on the public sector (described in sections 5 through 9, below) or the communal sector (described in 1, above).

As has been demonstrated by Coase, assuming income effects are negligible, the final allocation of resources devoted to water pollution abatement and the consequent allocation of resources devoted to goods X and Y (that is, the amount of X and Y society ends up with together with the amount of pollution abatement) is independent of the initial assignment of rights or liability -- this a simple restatement of the Coase Theorem.[2] As long as the government explicitly does or does not make the chemical firm liable, (that is, explicitly assigns the rights to the farmer or assigns them to the chemical firm, respectively) the ensuing market bargaining process will serve to efficiently internalize the negative externality.

Figure V.2 can be used to describe the relationship between the assignment of rights, the incentives created, and the consequent behavior of the parties of interest so as to generate an efficient solution under this particular environmental economic remedy. We continue to assume that individual X is the farmer and thus the victim of the pollution while Y, the chemical firm, is the source of the pollution. The line labeled MBx represents the marginal benefit to the farmer when additional units of pollution abatement are undertaken; the line labeled MCy represents the marginal costs to the chemical firm of increased pollution abatement. If transactions costs are zero, then, as Coase made clear, whether or not the chemical firm is liable for the damages caused -- that is, whether the farmer or the chemical firm is granted the right by the government -- the bargaining outcome will result in the same amount of pollution abatement -- the Pareto efficient X*. That is, the amount of pollution abatement is invariant over different assignments of rights or liability.

It is important to understand the link between the change in rights, the consequent change in economic incentives, and the altered behavior of the two parties of interest. In Figure V.2, if the government initially decides that the chemical firm is not liable for the damages caused to the farmer, bargaining would begin at point A (no abatement and 100% pollution). For the first unit, the marginal benefit to the farmer of one unit of pollution abatement ($a) is clearly greater than the marginal cost of abatement by the chemical firm ($b); therefore, the farmer would incrementally bribe the chemical firm to produce some abatement. Conceptually, the amount of the bribe would be something greater than $b and perhaps less than $a with the actual outcome being a function of the relative bargaining skills of the two parties. This same incremental bribe process would continue for the next unit, since $c is greater than $d, the chemical firm will once again abate its pollution...etc. until point X* is reached. The essential point here is that the chemical firm, under the government imposed rights structure (with the chemical firm not liable), would perceive the farmer's bribe as part of the opportunity costs of producing good Y and therefore, when taken into consideration, internalizes the externality. Beyond X*, the level of pollution is causing too little crop damage, yielding a marginal bribe by the farmer equal only to $f, insufficient to cause the chemical firm to engage in any further abatement, since the latter's marginal cost $e is now greater than $f.

Alternatively, if the government had instead placed liability on the chemical firm (i.e., granted the rights to the farmer), bargaining would begin at point B (100% abatement and no pollution). For the potential last unit of pollution abatement, the marginal cost to the chemical firm $g is very high while the marginal benefit of that last unit of abatement to the farmer of an almost pristine river is very low, $h. Accordingly, the chemical firm will have every incentive to incrementally bribe the farmer to be able to pollute. That is, the farmer will accept incremental bribes from the chemical firm allowing the firm to dump its effluents into the river as long as $g exceeds $h, $i exceeds $j...etc. and proceed to X* -- the same Pareto-efficient solution as above.

As is evident, under the assumption of zero transactions costs, the bargaining process may be used to internalize the externality as long as the government acts to transfer the river from common property to private property by either assigning the right to the chemical firm *or* to the farmer. As such, when the chemical firm is deciding on its production decision with respect to good Y, it will take into account either (a) if liable -- the payments it must make to the farmer as a result of disposing its effluents into the river, or (b) if not liable -- the foregone payments from the farmer who stands ready to bribe the chemical firm for not increasing its pollution. Thus, the Coase bargaining solution is one method of internalizing the negative externality that can bring about the Pareto optimal solution X* regardless to whom the liability is assigned with the allocative results independent of the initial assignment of rights.

(3) The Coase Solution -- Positive Transactions Costs

In the case of positive transactions costs, to simplify matters, it is assumed that once the government assigns the right to one party, the other party bears the burden of the transactions costs (hereafter, this will be referred to as the "TC" assumption). Thus, in Figure V.3 (at base, the same as Figure V.2), MB'x depicts the marginal benefits of additional units of pollution abatement to the farmer adjusted for transactions costs (i.e., a net reduction in marginal benefits) when the chemical firm is granted the right by the government, that is, when not liable. When the chemical firm is granted the right and the farmer must bear the transactions costs [under the "TC" assumption], the farmer's maximum incremental bribes to the chemical firm will be reduced by the amount of the transactions costs it must incur.

Alternatively, MC'y is the chemical firm's marginal costs incurred for enhanced pollution abatement adjusted for transactions costs when the farmer is granted the right, that is, when the government decides that the chemical firm is to be liable. It should be clear that if the farmer is granted the right and the chemical firm must bear the transactions costs [under the "TC" assumption], the chemical firm's maximum incremental bribes to the farmer will be reduced by the amount of the transactions costs it must incur. In addition, for expositional purposes, it is also assumed here that the transactions costs for the chemical firm are greater than the transactions costs for the farmer.

If rights are initially assigned to the chemical firm (i.e., the chemical firm is not liable), the bargaining process will begin at point A (no abatement, 100% pollution). Through incremental bribes by the farmer (bribes now reduced in value by the fact that the farmer must incur the transactions costs ["TC"]), as described earlier, the farmer will bribe the chemical firm as $a exceeds $b, $c exceeds $d,...etc. to get the chemical firm to abate its polluting activity. The bargaining will proceed to point C along curve MB'x (where MB'x = MCy) yielding X' level of pollution abatement. Alternatively, if the farmer is assigned the right (i.e., the chemical firm is liable for the damages caused), bargaining commences at point B (zero pollution, 100% abatement). Now the chemical firm will incrementally bribe the farmer to allow it to deposit some effluents into the river (with bribes now reduced in value by the fact that the chemical firm must incur the transactions costs ["TC"]) as $e exceeds $f, $g exceeds $h,...etc. The bargaining proceeds to point D along curve MC'y (where MC'y = MBx) yielding X" level of pollution abatement -- quite different than X'.

As is evident, it is the existence of transactions costs that does not allow the bargaining process to yield the Pareto efficient solution X*. However, inasmuch as X' is closer to the efficient solution X* than is X", then the normative implication for government policy is that the rights structure associated

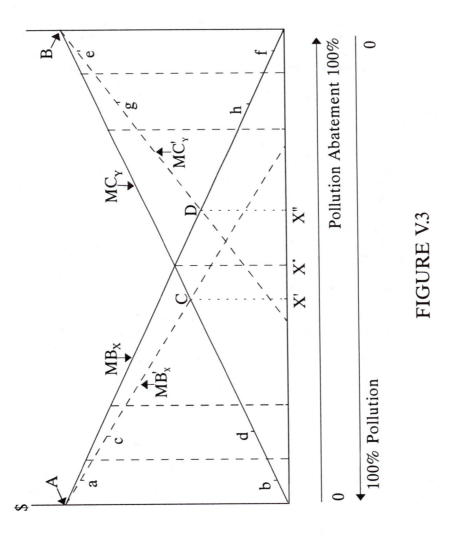

FIGURE V.3

with X' is said to be preferred to the alternative rights structure associated with X". It follows then that, in general, the party that has the greater transactions costs should be given the right; in this example, the chemical firm should not be made liable. It is important to note that given the assumptions in this example, the solution is in direct contrast to the conventional progressive tradition of legal reformers and the Pigouvians both of whom would act to restrain the chemical firm -- but, as this example is constructed, the chemical firm is instead given the right.

The economic logic that is suggested is that from society's standpoint, by giving the rights to the party (the chemical firm) that would otherwise bear large transactions costs, the lower-transactions cost party (the farmer) must bear the transactions costs burden of internalization (and thereby avoid that unnecessary larger transactions costs expenditure). The logic of this reasoning is inherent in Coase's approach where he states:

> The problem which we face in dealing with actions which have harmful effects is not simply one of restraining those responsible for them. What has to be decided is whether the gain from preventing the harm is greater than the loss which would be suffered elsewhere as a result of stopping the action which produces the harm. In a world in which there are costs of rearranging the rights established by the legal system, the courts, in cases relating to nuisance, are in effect, making a decision on the economic problem and determining how resources are to be employed. It was argued that the courts are conscious of this and that they often make, although not always in a very explicit fashion, a comparison between what would be gained and what would be lost by preventing actions which have harmful effects (Coase, 1960:27-28).

What this suggests, with reference to Figure V.3, is that the courts should consider (through implicit approximation) MBx and MCy in an attempt to arrive at point X*. However, it should be apparent that the courts may not be perfect evaluators of all the relevant costs and benefits and, as a result, the court determined solution (X' or X") may differ from X*. But as the logic of efficiency suggests, if one cares about "what would be gained and what would be lost," it makes sense in this case for the court to grant the right to the chemical firm (i.e., not make it liable for the damages caused to the farmer).

As has been demonstrated, if rights to perform certain actions can be bought and sold under zero transactions costs, then they will tend to be acquired by those for whom they are most valuable -- either in production or in the enhancement of utility in consumption -- the outcome will be that which yields the greatest value on the market. But as shown, the existence of transactions costs can inhibit those trades, bargains, and contractual arrangements that would be necessary to achieve the efficient solution. The normative thrust of the economic approach to law suggests that, in disputed cases, the court should assign the property rights to the party who would be willing to pay the most to obtain them if rights could have been exchanged without costs. Since the transactions costs could be so high so as to prevent the transfer of rights, it makes sense for the court to place the rights with the party that values them the most. It is in this sense that the economic approach is characterized as approximating a market solution. But again, as Coase stated, "The problem which we face in dealing with actions which have harmful effects is not simply one of restraining those responsible for them." While restraining the emitter may serve as a psychic balm for some, Coase simply suggests that given the economic considerations, the world is a bit more complex.

(4) Conglomerate Firm

The conglomerate firm represents yet another potential remedy by which to have the negative externality internalized within the private market sector. Instead of having the river held as a common property resource, under the conglomerate firm as a remedy, the property rights structure is such that either (1) the chemical firm acquires the downstream farm, (2) the downstream farm acquires the chemical firm, or (3) a third party acquires both of these separate entities and organizes them into a conglomerate firm. Notwithstanding which one of these three options is exercised, the new rights structure alters the incentives confronting the firm's owner/manager and channels its behavior resulting in an efficient allocation of society's scarce resources.

Once the conglomerate firm is established, the manager of the profit maximizing conglomerate firm would have to decide whether the marginal production of more chemical products, at the direct cost to the same conglomerate firm's farm yield, was worth it. That is, the additional production of chemicals may result in a level of incremental water pollution that now damages the conglomerate firm's farm products. Under this new rights structure, the question confronting the firm's owners is -- Does the value of the additional chemical products exceed or fall short of the value of the damage to the firm's farm products?

As described by Coase, the conglomerate firm represents an institutional alternative wherein "for a market transaction is substituted an administrative decision."[3] (Coase, 1960:16). On this point Coase stated:

> Although production could be carried out in a completely
> decentralized way by means of contracts, between individuals, the
> fact that it costs something to enter into these transactions means
> that the firms will emerge to organize what would otherwise be
> market transactions whenever their costs were less than the costs
> of carrying out the transactions through the market (Coase,
> 1988:7).

Clearly, the effect of the administrative solution is such that the negative
externality is internalized, and, with the optimal level of abatement of pollution,
the resources would be efficiently allocated between chemical and farm products.
As further observed by Coase, it would make sense to adopt the conglomerate
firm solution "whenever the administrative costs of the firm were less than the
costs of the market transactions that it supersedes and the gains which would
result from the rearrangement of activities greater than the firm's costs of
organization" (Coase, 1960:17).

(5) Enforce the Relevant Common Law

a. An Introduction to the Nature of Common Law and Its Relation to
Doctrinalism -- Common law can be said to consist of the rules that emanate from
the principles and doctrines developed gradually by judges originally of the
English royal courts as the foundation of their decisions. In the U.S., its force
and authority emanates from that portion of the common law of England
(including those acts of the parliament) that were applicable and had been adopted
and in force at the time of the American revolution. So far as it has not since
been expressly abrogated, the common law is recognized as an organic part of the
jurisprudence of most of the U.S. Over time, judges of various jurisdictions
(from England to America) have added to and continue to recognize the authority
of the accumulating body of common law. Classical common law thought
continues to be perceived as an internally, coherent, unified body of principles
and doctrines -- principles and doctrines that comprise the substrate upon which
the decision rules of common law rest and derive their authority from usages and
customs, as well as from the decrees and judgements of the courts in affirming
those usages and customs.

A point to be emphasized is that while common law resides in judicial
decisions, in classical common law *something* stands behind the judicial decisions.
That something serves to justify the judicial decisions, helps guide the law's
development, helps provide a unity and autonomy to the common law, and
finally, that something gives the law its authority. That something is the fact that

the law is grounded in, and logically derived from, a handful of general principles and doctrines.

b. Doctrinalism -- It was in the 1870s when Christopher Columbus Langdell, the Dean of Harvard Law School, institutionalized the doctrinal concept as the appropriate way to think about the law. He accomplished this by promoting law as an academic undertaking -- arguing that law should be recognized as one of the specialized disciplines within the university (and not relegated to the law office instruction of law clerks). Langdell succeeded in establishing two things: first that law was a science; and second that all of the available materials of this science are contained in books and cases documenting over 500 years of legal decisions.

The Langdellian tradition -- or as it has come to be know *doctrinalism* -- argues that law ought to be a deductive and autonomous science; a self-contained undertaking in the sense that particular legal decisions follow from the application of fundamental legal principles and doctrines. From the Langdellian vantage point, the task of the legal scholar and student of law is that of inferring from the entire body of "judge-made case law" the "appropriate" or "true" rules, doctrines, and procedures consistent with intelligible, fundamental legal principles that constitute the heart of common law. The academic side of law is then the process of uncovering the fundamental principles that weave their way through the common law over time -- principles that provide the foundation for legal decisions that give rise to rules and procedures without regard to values and always outside any social, economic, or political context.

Whole subject areas in the present law school curriculum, for example, contracts, torts, and property have their boundaries fixed and are distinguished from each other by their respective common law principles. Indeed, in the classical common law tradition, today much of legal education and legal scholarship consists of the exposition and systematization of these general principles and the techniques required to find and apply them together with the legal rules, doctrines and procedures that emanate therefrom.

According to the declaratory doctrine of common law, "judges do not make law; they do not create it; they interpret and apply the law." In deciding cases, the judge expresses part of the total, immanent wisdom of law (a wisdom existing only in one's mind) which is assumed to be preexistent before the judge's decision. The judge works from within the law -- within the repository of the experience of the community over time -- within a community imbued with its own culture and customs. It is the judge's immanent wisdom of the community's culture and customs over time that lends both authority and legitimacy to the common law. Inasmuch as the common law is seen to be residing in the community and not the political arena, the emergent legal order comes to command the highest respect. If instead the judge had *made* the law and thereby imposed that law on a community as if he were a political ruler or the servant of one, this would undermine his authority inasmuch as a judge's authority is based on his being a representative of the community and, as its representative, only able to *state* the community's law -- not *make* the community's law.

c. The Doctrine of Precedent -- The common law doctrine of precedent must be understood vis-a-vis the concept of legal change. The doctrine of precedent states that judges are bound to treat as binding on them the essential legal grounds of decisions adopted in similar cases previously adjudicated in courts of higher (or perhaps equal) status. A judge must attach great weight to previous decisions -- a principle which opts more for continuity than it does for legal change.

One must keep in mind that at any moment in time, common law decisions, in general, reflect the best available evidence of the collective wisdom of the common law judges. However, the common law is comprised of fundamental principles that are expressions of the culture and customs of the society. The latter are not frozen in time but change -- perhaps only incrementally -- but nonetheless change. Consequently, the common law, as an expression of culture and custom also can change. That is, legal change in the common law comes about not so much in spite of the fact that a judge is bound by a previous legal decision, but because a judge is bound to the principles implicit and explicit within the changing culture and customs of a society -- and any past legal decision is seen as subordinate to the more fundamental emergent common law principles.

d. A Process Perspective of Today's Law -- For our purposes here, the *law* can be seen to be comprised of the entire outcome of the ongoing legal process. That is, the law can be conceived of as (1) the prevailing constitution, (2) the present entire body of statutes, and (3) the current legal rules inscribed into the common law (based on common law principles and doctrines as described above). From this vantage point, the state (a) structures political and legal institutions with the adoption of their respective working rules, (b) creates (dis)incentives, and thereby (c) channels behavior within the choice-making processes of these institutions. From the combined structure and consequent behavior of these choice-making institutions, over time, the law continuously emerges.

In simple terms, the prevailing working rules that structure the political, judicial, and administrative institutions channel the political, judicial, and administrative decision-making -- perhaps eclectically, it channels governmental decision making. The combined outcome of these political/legal/administrative institutions yields, at any one moment in time, the prevailing (1) the common law rules and doctrines, (2) presidential and governors' executive orders, (3) federal and state legislative statutes, together with (4) the whole plethora of commission and agency rules and government regulations, the total sum of which we have termed the *legal relations governing society* -- or simply the *law.*

e. The Common Law and the Environment -- In modern legal practice a tort is the word used to denote a wrongful act for which a legal action will lie. It is distinguished from the relevant set of issues inherent in contract law, property law, and criminal law. Before 1970, individual states attempted to control the acts of polluters with a heavy reliance on the common law of torts. This area of law is primarily concerned with the duty to avoid causing harm to others. In resolving pollution cases the judges relied on the common law doctrines of negligence, nuisance, and trespass, as well as strict liability for abnormally dangerous activities. The liability rules that developed within the common law were not originally concerned with damage to natural resources, the environment, or with ecosystem preservation. However, the extent to which damage to the environment may be incidental to injuries to person and property, modern common law liability rules are relevant to these concerns (Schoenbaum, 1985: 33). Parties injured by the negative externalities caused by others have recourse to four common law doctrines.

(i) Nuisance -- The traditional common law tort doctrine that is most closely related to issues regarding the environment is nuisance -- most typically noise, water, and air pollution. Nuisance is defined as the class of wrongs that arise from to the unreasonable, unwarrantable, or unlawful use by a person of his own property, either real or personal, or from his own improper, indecent, or unlawful personal conduct, causing an obstruction of or injury to the right of another or of the public, and producing such material annoyance, inconvenience, discomfort, or hurt that the law will presume resulting damage.[4] The general rule is that a person may use his/her land in any manner (s)he sees fit, but not to cause injury or annoyance to his/her neighbor. In determining whether a given act constitutes a nuisance, the court will consider the act itself, the place, and the circumstances surrounding the act; that act must materially affect the physical comfort of ordinary people under normal circumstances or conditions.

There are two kinds of nuisances, private and public. A private nuisance -- an interference with the use and enjoyment of the land of another -- may be abated by an injunction brought by the affected party. On the other hand, a public nuisance, typically affects an indefinite number of people, and constitutes an unreasonable interference with the interests of the community or rights of the general public. A public nuisance is normally abated by a public official.

In order to establish a private nuisance a plaintiff must show "substantial" injury measured in terms of economic harm as a result of unreasonable conduct on the part of the defendant. Two of the more prominent defenses to nuisance actions are (a) coming to nuisance, and (b) balancing the equities. The coming to nuisance defense is quite straight forward. This defense can be used by a person sued or prosecuted wherein (s)he claims that the complainant (or plaintiff) affected by the nuisance moved into the area where the activity had long been in existence.

From the standpoint of economics, balancing the equities has greater relevance. The question here centers on the reasonableness of the defendant's conduct. The determination of reasonableness is in the balancing of the 'gravity of the harm' versus the 'utility of the defendant's conduct.' The process is one of balancing the rights of property owners each asserting their right to use their land in a manner which conflicts with the right of the other party, (that is, to weight the harm done to the injured party against the economic benefits of the damaging activity [akin to Kaldor-Hicks efficiency]). In this latter regard, nuisance law can internalize external costs by establishing such criteria as (a) whether a violation of property rights has occurred, (b) who is liable for the damage, and (c) assessing the amount of the damages/liability.[5] If the act is found to be a tort, the court must then apply the appropriate remedy, either issuing an injunction against the activity or provide equity relief requiring the payment of compensatory damages.

(ii) Trespass -- The common law tort doctrine defines trespass as an unauthorized and direct breach of the boundaries on another's land.[6] That is, the polluting activity must constitute an interference with a landowner's right to exclusive possession -- generally, there must be a physical invasion of the property. The common law recognizes three types of trespass that have some relevance to issues regarding the environment: trespass to personal property (the destruction or the taking of another's property), trespass to the person (a physical act committed on a person), and trespass to reality. It is the latter that has the most significant link to environmental issues. In an action for trespass to reality, entry upon another's land may be made by causing or permitting a thing to cross the boundary of the premises -- for example, the depositing (casting) of materials, the discharging of water or other liquids, or the discharging of soot.

(iii) Negligence and Strict Liability -- The common law doctrine of negligence requires that the party allegedly responsible for the polluting activity owes a duty to the affected party (the plaintiff) to exercise due care. If the court finds that duty has been breached, the polluter is found negligent and required to compensate the plaintiff for the damages caused. Typically the test employed to determine if the plaintiff has exercised due care is the *Learned Hand Formula* (named after Supreme Court Justice, Learned Hand). The formula (fundamentally consistent with economic theory) states that the polluter is guilty of negligence if the loss caused by the pollution , multiplied by the probability of the pollution occurring, exceeds the cost of preventing the pollution before hand.

Alternatively, in many places, the doctrine of negligence has been supplemented by the doctrine of strict liability. Under this doctrine the party affected by the pollution may not have to prove negligence. As long as a *dangerous activity* caused the damage, the polluter is declared liable. Strict lability can be consistent with efficiency particular in cases dealing with inherently dangerous and hazardous products. By imposing strict liability for this class of activities where the likelihood of serious damage would be very high, the would-be defendant would a priori take much greater precautions to avoid the dangerous impacts and the accompanying damage awards than (s)he would under a rule of negligence. On the other hand, where the likelihood of serious damage is not great, but the burdens of precaution are substantial, the rule of negligence is efficiency enhancing.

f. Efficiency of the Common Law -- One the pervasive themes in the literature in the field of the *new law & economics* is the purported efficiency of the common law. Proponents of this line of literature refer to it as "the positive branch of the economic theory of law." This concept was systematically explored by Coase in a *The Problem of Social Costs* (Coase, 1960) and then taken up and extended by Richard A. Posner among others (Posner, 1986). Simply stated, it is the hypothesis that the development of the common law can be explained *as if* its goal was to maximize allocative efficiency. That is, the basic thesis is that the common law (especially the law of torts) is best explained *as if* the judges who created the law through decisions operating as precedents, in latter cases were trying to promote efficient resource allocation (Landes and Posner, 1987:1).

It must be underscored that the extent to which the proponents of this line of reasoning succeed in having it gain acceptance, it will serve as an ideological barrier to the general promotion of statutory law -- more specifically, a barrier to the passing of statutes dedicated to maintaining the ecological integrity of the natural system. The logic underlying the "efficiency of the common law" thesis generally follows the following contour: Whenever the market falls a bit short of providing an efficient allocation of resources due to environmental externalities, the proponents of "the efficiency of common law" contend the answer lies in relying on the common law and damage measures (a common law they purport to have demonstrated to be comprised of doctrines and rules that produce efficient results) to give the ever willing market a gentle nudge in the direction of maximum social welfare. Thus, given the existence of negative environmental externalities, society need not rely on the ever-ready legislative branch to either pass environmental statutes, or to have the bureaucracy adopt environmentally favorable working rules or status rights which are not inherently efficient -- all one needs to do is rely on the efficient common law.

g. Least-Cost Avoider Rules -- The unearthing of the efficiency of the common law is thought to be particularly evident in the field of tort law (though, it must be noted that much of the literature purports to offer evidence confirming the view that there is an efficiency of common law doctrines in the fields of contract and other areas). Here the subtle shift from the positive (description) to the normative (prescription) takes place. If society has an array of liability rules from which to pick (say rules that may lead to the reduction of accidents or the abating of polluting activities), then the economic logic suggests you choose the least cost alternative.

This line of reasoning was originally presented by Guido Calabressi coincidentally, at about the same time Coase authored *The Problem of Social Costs.*[7] The logic inherent in the literature on efficient liability rules is based upon three suppositions: (1) that all loses can be expressed in monetary terms; (2) that the undesirable accidents or pollution can be reduced by devoting more of society's scarce resources to the accident prevention or pollution abatement; and (3) that those individuals who are potentially involved in accidents or polluting activities are sensitive to cost pressures.

The economic logic of this approach can be expressed with two simple examples. The first is to let Figure V.4 represent all of the costs associated with say, automobile accidents (including the actual damages suffered by victims, litigation expenses, legal administrative costs, enforcement costs,...etc.) before the government acts in an attempt to reduce society's costs of accidents. Assume the government first installs traffic signals and stop signs with perhaps, the net savings to society being the area beneath line AA. Now assume, additionally that the government erects costly median barriers with again some net savings to society this time equal to the area ABBA. The area above line BB represents the residual costs of accidents -- or as they are commonly referred to, the *interaction damage costs*. It is these costs that are the focus of the literature on economics of liability rules.

The economic approach to the analysis and selection of liability rules can be viewed as one method by which risks in society are taken to be *background risks* with the costs borne by the victim; or alternatively, *compensated risks* which arise from tortuous acts with the costs being borne by the injurer. The primary focus of the economic approach to liability rule formulation, is to develop a standard of liability that minimizes the sum total of interaction damage costs under the full recognition that the selection of a specific liability rule will determine which actions will fall within the scope of background risks versus those actions that will be deemed compensated risks. Focusing only on the

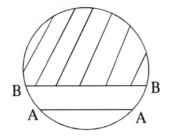

FIGURE V.4

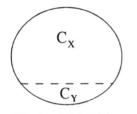
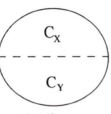
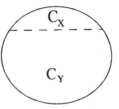

Limited Liability
Rule

Negligence
Rule

Strict Liability
Rule

FIGURE V.5

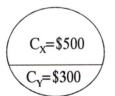
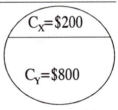

Limited Liability
Rule

Negligence
Rule

Strict Liability
Rule

FIGURE V.6

interaction damage costs (the shaded area above line BB in Figure V.4 which is now equal to the area of each of the three circles in Figure V.5), we can easily describe the two facets of the problem.

First, in each panel of Figure V.5, let Cx represent all costs borne by victims because the liability rule chosen considers the risks associated with these interaction damage costs as part of the background risks in society. In a like manner, in each panel let Cy represent all compensable costs borne by the injurers because the liability rule chosen considers the risks associated with these interaction damage costs as tortious and not part of background risks. As is evident, depending upon which liability rule becomes part of the legal relations governing society, either more or less risks are taken to be background risks and therefore less or more compensable, respectively. That is, with the hypothetical limited liability rule, most risks are considered background risks and most injurers are not liable for the damages caused (the victims bear most of the costs). Alternatively, at the other extreme using strict liability, most risks are not considered background risks with the injurers being liable for most of the damages caused. Perhaps somewhere between the two lies a third liability rule, a hypothetical negligence rule, that establishes a system under which injurers are liable for the damages only if negligent (i.e., at fault). The fundamental point illustrated here is that the choice of one liability rule over another results in a different distribution of costs for society. It is only for expositional purposes that the three circles have the same area (i.e., represent the same interaction damage costs). Indeed, as stated above, the thrust of the economic approach to liability rule formulation is to develop a standard of liability that minimizes the sum total of interaction damage costs. Figure V.6 illustrates the economic approach that attempts to inform society of the efficiency consequences of the choice of one liability rule over another.

Hypothetically, let us say that the limited liability rule results in most costs ($500 = 62.5\%$) being borne by the victims with some costs ($300 = 37.5\%$) being paid for in damages. With the limited liability rule we observe the total size of the interaction damage costs equal to $800. Alternatively, suppose the strict liability rule results in a different distribution of costs with most costs, (say $800 = 80\%$) being borne by the injurers with only few costs ($200 = 20\%$) going uncompensated being borne by the victims. Here, the total size of the interaction damage costs equal to $1,000. Finally, for the rule of negligence, this rule yields a distribution of costs where some $240 = 40\%$ are borne by the injurers and $360 = 60\%$ of the costs going uncompensated being borne by the victims. Importantly, the total size of the interaction damage costs is equal to $600. Based on a simple comparison, the economic approach would suggest adopting the hypothetical negligence liability rule (as $600 is less than both $800 and $1,000). It should be noted that the explicit adoption of the least-cost solution carries with it the implicit adoption (perhaps "legitimation") of the specific distribution of risk that goes along with that least-cost chosen rule -- *justice* and *fairness* aside. Note that while the conventional approach to tort law centers on questions of justice and/or fairness as related to questions of risk and costs, this conventional approach is at direct odds with the economic approach that advocates the adoption of "efficient" rules. These two remain in dispute. The tension that exists between these two approaches is clearly evident in the following two quotes:

> Since the efficient use of resources is an important although not always paramount social value, the burden, I suggest, is on the authors to present reasons why a standard that appears to impose avoidable costs on society should nonetheless be adopted. They have not carried this burden. (Posner, 1973:221).

> Once it is admitted that there are questions of fairness as between the parties that are not answerable in economic terms, the exact role of economic argument in the solution of legal questions becomes impossible to determine. It may well be that an acceptable theory of fairness can be reconciled with the dictates of economic theory in a manner that leaves ample room for the use of economic thought. But that judgement presupposes that some theory of fairness has been spelled out, which once completed, may leave no room for economic considerations of any sort. (Epstein, 1973:152)

An alternative way of illustrating the economic approach to liability formulation is as follows. Let us suppose that legal policy makers have come up with five different liability rules that can help diminish accidents or polluting activities. Each of the five liability rules corresponds to five different damage awards to the victims (#1 lowest damage award --> #5 the highest damage award). In addition, each liability rule induces a different level of care (from #1 none --> #5 extreme). The aim of efficiency-based tort law is to use damage awards after the event to replace what may be termed "the unfeasible agreements" that would have occurred had a market been possible. The *Total Costs* are equal to the sum of the *Cost of Care* plus the *Expected Accident Costs*. It should be clear from the simple example that a system of efficiency-based tort law ought to include the most efficient -- least-cost avoider liability rule #3 -- that rule which minimizes the total costs of accidents or pollution at $16.

Liability Rules	Individuals' Level of Care	Cost of Care	Accident Prob'ity	Expected AcLosses	Total Costs
#1	none	$ 0	% 15	$ 20	$ 20
#2	low	$ 2	% 11	$ 16	$ 18
#3	moderate	$ 5	% 7	$ 11	$ 16
#4	high	$ 9	% 4	$ 8	$ 17
#5	extreme	$ 14	% 1	$ 5	$ 19

(6) Regulation Through the Constitution -- A Public Choice Approach

a. Catallaxy -- Public choice theory is defined the application of economic analysis to political decision making, including theories of the state, voting rules and voter behavior, apathy, party politics, log rolling, bureaucratic choice, policy analysis, and regulation.[8] It constitutes an approach to environmental questions that focuses predominately on the creation and implementation of law through the political process, as opposed to the common-law as described above.

Public choice theory is concerned with political processes and, as such, can be viewed as an "opening up" of the conventional neoclassical economic paradigm, where political processes are typically taken as given. As with market exchange, the motive for agreement in political exchange is mutual advantage and the gains from trade that are garnered from participation. At the same time, public choice theory can be understood as a movement towards "closure" with respect to the nature of the analysis.

From the methodological perspective, public choice represents a movement toward the analysis of closed systems (Buchanan, 1972). In neoclassical economics, political institutions, political decision makers, and thus political decisions are perceived as *exogenous* to economic activity, whereas in public choice theory the institutions and decisions are *endogenous*. That is, rational, utility-maximizing individuals do not act solely in the marketplace where goods, services, and factors of production are exchanged, and through this market-exchange process, exhaust the gains from trade. These same individuals also participate in the political decision-making processes to enhance their utility. Consequently, society's scarce resources are allocated by both the marketplace and the political process -- by the same individuals acting in several separate capacities. James M. Buchanan has described this methodological movement toward closure as follows:

> The critically important bridge between the behavior of persons who act in the marketplace and the behavior of persons who act in political process must be analyzed. The 'theory of public choice' can be interpreted as the construction of such a bridge. The approach requires only the simple assumption that the same individuals act in both relationships. Political decisions are not handed down from on high by omniscient beings who cannot err. Individuals behave in market interactions, in political-government interactions, in cooperative-nongovernmental interactions, and in other arrangements. *Closure of the behavioral system*, as I am using the term, means only that analysis must be extended to the actions of persons in their several separate capacities.[9] [emphasis added] (Buchanan, 1972:12).

In the contractarian branch of public choice theory -- more typically, catallaxy -- the concepts of spontaneous coordination and spontaneous order take center stage. The emphasis shifts from simple to complex exchanges, that is, to all processes of voluntary agreements among persons in political as well as economic arenas. The central thrust of catallaxy is to take individual decision makers as the basic unit of analysis and to view both politics and the political processes in terms of the exchange paradigm.[10] At the most basic level, this approach is concerned with the constitutional stage of choice where the basic rules of collective order are resolved, while at a more intermediate level the discussion concerns the determination of the structure of government institutions (Buchanan, 1975:228). Hence, catallaxy represents the extension of the economic perspective to institutional settings in which persons interact collectively. Simply put, within the context of politics and political decision making, the role of the economist is to search out, invent, and broker social (re)arrangements which will embody Pareto-superior moves.

To this end, public choice theory focuses on the potential for complex exchange in the political arena under the rules of (1) unanimous consent (to ensure Pareto-superior results), and (2) the compensation requirement (i.e., Kaldor-Hicks efficiency).[11] Its essential thrust is to structure a political process where values are revealed through the political actions of individuals, and consensus among the individuals of the choosing group becomes the sole affirmation of social value. Like the market, political institutions are to be structured around the common unifying principle of gains-from-trade with a prescriptive focus on cost-minimizing rights structures together with conflict resolution by contracted agreements, vote-trading, vote selling, package deals, compensation, and compromise (Reisman, 1990:176).

The catallactic approach to public choice envisions the economist as proffering a social policy solution (or solutions) as "presumptively efficient" (that is, as a tentative hypothesis that a proposed solution is efficient) and then observing whether the solution finds support through the consensus of the individuals in the society. To the extent that a presumptively efficient policy (structured around inclusive, complex trading and exchange agreements) can garner unanimous agreement, the proponents of the catallactic approach can unambiguously recommend that particular policy -- in this case, an environmental policy.

b. Unanimous Consent, Pareto Optimality, and the Optimal Majority -- At the constitutional stage of choice, where the basic "rules of the game" are being adopted, catallaxy begins with the proposition that only the rule of unanimous consent should be used to adopt subsequent laws or to select policy (for each different category of government policy -- for this chapter, environmental policy), since only then can we be ensured that changes constitute movements to a Pareto-better state. However, it is recognized that a unanimity rule is costly -- these costs being the sum of (i) the *external costs of decision making* 'EC' and (ii) *the decision-making costs* 'DM'(See Figure V.7). With N as the total number of persons in the decision-making group, EC is a decreasing function since fewer and fewer costs can be imposed on external parties as we consider adopting decision rules (with # as the number of persons required to pass an environmental initiative) which come closer and closer to the unanimous consent requirement where # = N); whereas DM is an increasing function since it is more and more costly to bring more and more individuals into the decision-making process as we consider adopting decision rules which come closer and closer to the unanimous consent requirement (where # = N). Given these two costs (the sum of which constitutes 'TC' in Figure V.8), at the constitutional stage of choice it then becomes necessary to determine for environmental policy, which decision rule (i.e., the rule that will determine the optimal size of the decision-making group) will minimize the sum of the two costs (the minimum point on the now familiar U-shaped cost curve TC. In departing from the unanimous consent requirement and selecting the "least-cost optimal majority" rule, society in effect selects the most efficient rule (Buchanan and Tullock, 1962:43-84).

It is in this sense that we can observe that a "rationally" (or perhaps more accurately, "economically") constructed constitution will allow for specific collective decisions to be made that do not meet the strict Pareto criterion. Viewed in isolation, a collective decision regarding the environment can be made that does not meet the strict unanimous consent requirement. However, when

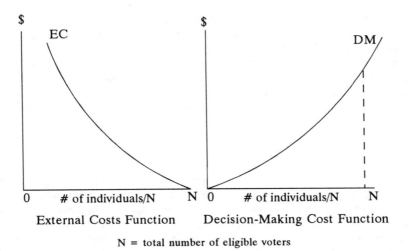

External Costs Function   Decision-Making Cost Function

N = total number of eligible voters

FIGURE V.7

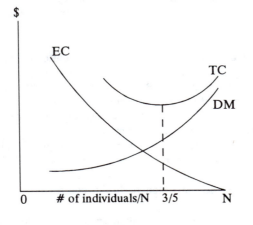

FIGURE V.8

viewed from a broader perspective, within the constitutional context, a collective decision as to which rule to use for issues regarding the environment does attain a legitimated status. It does so because, while the decision may not be Pareto efficient (here requiring only say a 3/5's vote instead of unanimous consent), the decision will have been made based on a rule that has the virtue of being cost minimizing; that is, it is a rule that *a priori* minimizes the sum of the external and decision-making costs to society. As such, it comes to command society's respect.

(7) Standards -- Regulations

For the past three decades, U.S. environmental regulatory programs have relied primarily on what we have termed status rights.[12] This regulation takes the form of a complex federal and state government command and control strategy where, in affect, the government holds the rights to the control and the regulated use of the environmental media. This selective status-right regulation allows producers and/or consumers to use the environment based on legal rules and agency orders to help improve or maintain the quality of the environment. The status rights that are established are based on standards that specify the conduct required of a class or category of economic actors.

Though it has varied over time, typically the government regulation approach requires several steps.

i. A designated pollution control agency (hereafter PCA) must be given the authority by the government (most often the legislature) to regulate the quality of the environment. By this action it makes explicit that the ecological integrity of the receiving environmental media will be regulated through use of status rights as opposed to relying on regulation through either the private sector or the communal sector.

ii. The PCA must determine the rules and regulations governing the behavior of each discharger (including such things as the installation of certain types of pollution control equipment...etc.) that are deemed necessary to achieve the stated pollution control goals or objectives or standards.

iii. The PCA must also establish a set of civil and perhaps criminal penalties or sanctions to be imposed on individuals or legal entities that are not in compliance with the stated regulations.

iv. The PCA must monitor the actions of dischargers so that the instances of noncompliance can be detected. Oftentimes this takes the form of a system of self-reporting with spot checks and environmental quality audits.

v. Finally, depending upon (a) the level of funding of the PCA's enforcement budget, (b) the severity or seriousness of violations of the regulations, and (c) the perceived willingness of a violator to work with the PCA to remedy existing pollution problems (perhaps through consent decrees if litigated in the courts)), the PCA may seek the additional aid of the courts to impose civil and criminal penalties on violators.

The specific standards set by the PCA can take two forms. One avenue of regulation is for the government agency to set specific standards that are typically based on governmental proscribed environmental quality *goals*. Once a goal is set, then the PCA proceeds to set specific standards in place -- standards that, as cumulatively met, go towards meeting the environmental quality goals. Alternatively, the more dominant approach is for the government to set nationally uniform technology-based effluent standards. Under this latter approach, each source, regardless of its circumstances (eg. its output, size, technology, location...etc.) is required to install and operate the best pollution control technology that is available and economically affordable. With respect to this latter approach, each plant or facility within an industry must meet the best available technology (BAT). The BAT requirements are usually promulgated as centralized uniform federal regulations with some considerations as to costs of coming into compliance. Exceptions may be made if the BAT requirements could result in shutting down the plant or economically jeopardize the industry.

With the setting of the standards, the regulation approach has as its aim to dictate specific across-the-board behavior by each plant or facility depositing residuals into the environment. It is a direct, across-the-board effort to control the quantity of pollution deposited into the natural system. It must be recognized that while there is nothing inherent within the regulatory system of the PCA to fashion a remedy that would be Pareto efficient, given the incentives that obtain under the specific status rights, there are important economic impacts that must be considered. The incidence of the costs associated with an across the board effluent standard can be observed in Figure V.9. As will be seen in a latter section of this chapter, the costs incurred under a *uniform effluent standard* are quite different than those that would be incurred with an *effluent charge*.

Specifically, let us assume that instead of one chemical firm, we have two upstream chemical firms, one on each side of the river -- firm A and firm B which have MC_A and MC_B, respectively, as their marginal costs of pollution abatement (where it is assumed that $MC_A < MC_B$). Assume further that without any PCA regulations, each firm would normally emit 600 units of effluents into the river each month.

If the PCA uniform effluent standard was to require each firm -- firms that have different marginal costs of pollution abatement -- to reduce its emissions by

two thirds (i.e., by 400 units per month), each firm's respective costs of abatement are indicated by the shaded areas. Thus, society would incur the sum of the two shaded regions (OABC + ODEF) to get 800 units of pollution abated. As will be seen below, the uniform approach described here, while treating each firm the same (perhaps "fairly"), does not take advantage of the potentially least-cost efficient solution associated with effluent charges or subsidies.

(8) Effluent Charges and Subsidies

As mentioned earlier in this chapter, there is a reformist tradition within both economics and law that suggests that in the event a situation arises where a negative externality is present and thereby resulting in market failure, the state should be called on for corrective government action. In such instances, it is typically thought that the state should take actions that will repress the activities of the emitter or the generator of the negative externality. The tradition was made explicit in the work of Arthur Pigou where he stated:

> But even in the most advanced States there are failures and imperfections. . . . there are many obstacles that prevent a community's resources from being distributed . . . in the most efficient way. The study of these constitutes our present problem. . . . its purpose is essentially practical. It seeks to bring into clearer light some of the ways in which it now is , or eventually may become, feasible for governments to control the play of economic forces in such wise as to promote the economic welfare, and through that, the total welfare, of their citizens as a whole (Pigou, [reprint] 1952:129-130).

Before proceeding with an analysis of the different economic incentives and outcomes that obtain under an effluent charge and a subsidy scheme, it is important to recognize the different implicit property rights assignments inherent in each scheme. In both cases the government (through its PCA) retains the rights over use of the environmental media. However, as will become evident as the analysis unfolds, when the PCA institutes a legislatively or administratively mandated effluent charge, implicitly, such a policy confers the right to use the environmental media to the party or parties who would otherwise experience the impact of the pollution (i.e., those upon whom the negative externality would be imposed). On the other hand, if the government's PCA is instead legislatively or administratively authorized to provide a subsidy to the discharger to abate its polluting activities, the implementation of the subsidy will implicitly transfer the right to use the environmental media to the discharger(s). Additionally, it will be demonstrated that under the conditions specified, both the effluent charge and the subsidy can be employed to internalize the negative externality and that both will result in the same allocatively efficient solution of pollution abatement; however, as we shall see, there will be a marked difference in the distributional effects of each policy.[13]

    a.   Effluent Charge[14] - In order to take advantage of the economic incentives that are inherent in an effluent charge, the PCA must do the following:

> i. The PCA must determine a set of prices per unit of waste discharge of each polluting substance with the price being an estimate of the per unit external costs of the polluting activity sufficient to induce the necessary abatement actions by the dischargers.
>
> ii. The PCA must also set up a system to comprehensively monitor for violations (or a system of self-reporting with spot checks and audits).
>
> iii. Finally, the PCA must collect a sum equal to the charge per unit of pollutants times the amount of the pollutant discharged during the reporting period.

    With the effluent charge, the government explicitly holds the rights to the environmental media. Returning to the simple example of the upstream chemical firm and the downstream farmer, the effluent charge places the implicit rights to use the river with the downstream farmer. To implement the scheme, the PCA must make an estimate of the per unit external costs of the polluting activity of the upstream chemical firm. This function translates into the marginal benefit function of the downstream farmer MB_F (see Figure V.10) . That is, MB_F represents the incremental benefits the farmer receives as the upstream chemical firm incrementally abates its pollution. For purposes of simplicity it is assumed in this example that MB_F is constant, though in reality it may be a diminishing function (consistent with the principle of diminishing marginal utility). MC_A represents the upstream chemical firm's marginal costs to incrementally abate its polluting activity. It is an increasing function by virtue of the law of diminishing returns.

    The incentives as well as the allocative and the distributive economic effects that result from the implicit rights structure associated with an effluent charge can be readily seen in Figure V.10. Specifically, assume the upstream chemical firm has OR units of waste discharge each month. Also assume that the PCA has accurately estimated that the per unit, monthly external cost of the pollution on the downstream farmer to be equal to $OC. Finally, MB_F (the

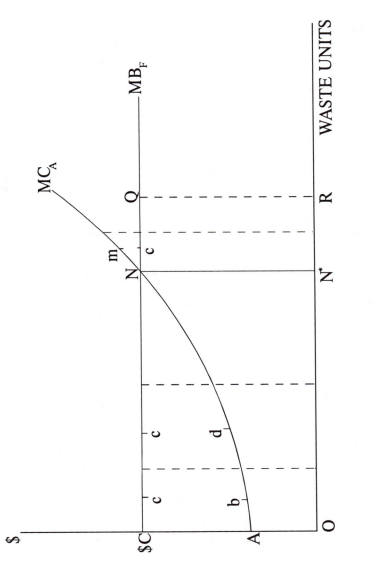

FIGURE V.10

marginal benefit of waste reduction to the farmer) and MC_A (the marginal cost of pollution abatement for the chemical firm) are given as described above.

With the effluent charge, we start out the analysis at point O where the chemical firm will have to incrementally decide whether, for the first unit of waste, to incur the marginal cost of abatement $b or pay the effluent charge $c; clearly the economic incentive dictates that the firm will select to abate the first unit of pollution. In a like manner, the firm will elect to abate the next unit at an incremental cost of $d as opposed to paying the effluent charge of $c... and so on, up to point N, finally abating ON^* units of pollution. Beyond point N the chemical firm will discharge its pollutants into the river and pay the incremental effluent charge $c (since $c is clearly less than $m, the marginal cost of abatement for the next unit beyond N^*). For all waste units beyond N^* out to R, the firm will discharge into the river but (since the farmer implicitly acquires the rights under the government imposed effluent charge remedy) the firm must pay the government the effluent charge at $c per unit for all units of waste discharged between N^* and R.

The costs incurred by society to attain ON^* units of pollution abatement are the sum of area $OANN^*$ dollars (the chemical firm's total costs of abatement for ON^* units of waste discharged) plus area N^*NQR dollars (the total sum of the effluent charge costs incurred by the chemical firm to potentially compensate society (in this limited case, the downstream farmer) for the external costs imposed. It is in this sense that the negative externality is seen to be internalized; the chemical firm must pay for the use of the river -- something that it would not be required to do if the river is held as a common property resource.

b. Subsidy - Alternatively, the legislature may elect to use a different structure of rights and thus an altered structure of economic incentives with the implementation of a subsidy program to attain the desired pollution abatement. Using the same Figure V.10, with a subsidy, the PCA is legislatively mandated to offer the chemical firm a maximum per unit subsidy equal to $c for each unit of waste units reduced. That is, starting at point O, for the first unit of waste to be discharged, the PCA would offer the chemical firm a unit subsidy of $c for not discharging the wastes into the river. Clearly, under this new structure of rights and hence economic incentives, the firm will elect to take the unit subsidy $c and incur the marginal cost $b to abate the first unit of waste discharge. In a like manner, as long as the marginal cost of pollution abatement is less than the subsidy offered by the PCA, the chemical firm will incrementally continue to accept the subsidy and, as in the case of the effluent charge, abate pollution from O to N resulting in ON^* units of abatement. Once beyond N^*, since the PCA's unit subsidy of $c is less than the marginal costs to further abate pollution $m, it is clearly in the interests of the chemical firm to exercise its implicit right to pollute the river (a right inherent in the subsidy scheme) and impose the external costs upon society (in this limited case, the downstream farmer).

The allocative and the distributive economic effects of the subsidy can clearly be observed in Figure V.10. The total costs to society include the total costs of abatement incurred by the chemical firm area OANN* dollars plus the sum of the external costs of area N*NQR imposed on the downstream farmer. It should be noted that the chemical firm's induced profit ACN can vary depending upon the extent to which the unit subsidy offered by the PCA exceeds the firm's marginal cost of abatement.

As is evident, both the effluent charge and the subsidy scheme result in the same level of optimal pollution abatement equal ON* and deposit the same optimal amount of discharges N*R into the river. However, a fundamental difference in economic incentives exists between the two schemes. In the former case, the chemical firm reacts to the potential economic penalty of the effluent charge realizing that it will have to pay either the one cost (pollution abatement cost) or the other (the effluent charge). In effect, by choosing to move along the AN segment of its MC curve, the profit maximizing chemical firm takes actions to minimize the impact on its net revenues by selecting the least-cost solution.

Alternatively, the subsidy offered to the chemical firm by the PCA to reduce its pollution represents an opportunity cost in terms of potential foregone revenue. That is, with the subsidy, the PCA is in affect offering a payment to the chemical firm not to exercise its implicit right to discharge into the environment. Thus, the profit maximizing firm will perceive "waste reduction" as a marketable good and, as demonstrated above, will incrementally accept the subsidy (as it is a form of revenue). Once beyond ON*, the chemical firm will exercise its right and elect to discharge into the environment -- that is, take those combined actions that maximize its net revenue position and, at the same time, internalize the negative externality.

     c.   A Comparison of the Uniform Effluent Standard Versus the Effluent Charge -- The differing economic impacts of a uniform effluent standard (analyzed above) versus an effluent charge can be demonstrated by comparing Figures V.9 and V.11. As will become evident, the costs incurred by society for the same amount of pollution abatement under an *uniform effluent standard* are quite different than those that would be incurred with an *effluent charge*.[15] Once again let us assume we have two chemical firms, A and B located up river from the farmer; each chemical firm emits 600 units of discharge into the environment per month; and due to their technologies, the two firms have different marginal costs of abatement ($MC_A < MC_B$). Finally, let us continue to assume that the goal of the PCA is to reduce pollution into the river by a total of 800 units per month. The extent to which the policy succeeds, society (in this limited case the

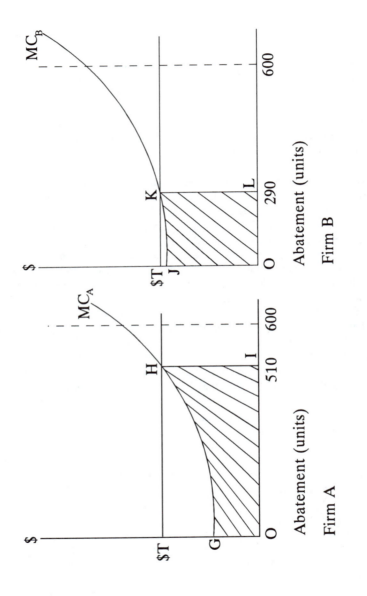

FIGURE V.11

farmer) receives the benefits of the PCA policy goal to reduce pollution into the river by 800 total units

As demonstrated earlier, if effluent standards are applied uniformly for similarly situated discharges which have different marginal costs of pollution abatement, then the total pollution abatement costs to society are the sum of the two shaded regions in Figure V.9. More specifically, if the PCA's across the board uniform effluent standard was to require each firm to reduce its emissions by two thirds (i.e., by 400 units per month), each firm's respective costs of abatement are indicated by the shaded areas OABC (total abatement costs for Firm A) + ODEF (total abatement costs for Firm B). However, the across the board, uniform approach, while treating each firm the same (perhaps "fairly"), does not take advantage of the potentially least-cost efficient solution associated with the effluent charge.

The legislature could instead have instructed the PCA to promulgate an effluent charge as the preferred instrument to achieve the government's environmental goal of reducing discharges by a total of 800 units in the region. The economic impact on society can be seen in Figure V.11. The PCA would have to implement an effluent charge at that level (in this case $T) where the sum of the two levels of abatement (510 units for firm A plus 290 units for firm B) equals its required total reduction level of 800 units. With the successful implementation of the effluent charge, society (in this limited case, the farmer) again receives the benefits of the PCA policy goal to reduce pollution into the river by 800 total units. However, under this scheme, the PCA policy to reduce pollution by 800 units is accomplished at a much reduced societal costs of abatement equal to shaded area OGHI (total abatement costs for Firm A) plus area OJKL (total abatement costs for Firm B). The reason society maintains the same level of pollution abatement benefits under both schemes but at a much lower cost with the effluent charge, is because the incentives inherent within the effluent charge. The nature of the effluent charge is such that it places a greater economic burden on those firms that can avoid polluting at a lower cost thereby saving society the otherwise unnecessary costs associated with a uniform effluent standard. In passing, it should be noted that the economic logic underlying the effluent charge follows the same economic logic of granting the right to the chemical firm when transactions costs were positive as well as the discussion of the "least-cost-avoider rule" both described earlier in this chapter. The effluent charge has additional two additional virtues: that of providing each individual firm the continuing incentive to find cheaper ways of abating pollution (by adopting new technologies) that shift down each firm's respective MC curve; and the extent to which the firm's effluents into the ecosystem exceeds the assimilative capacity to absorb the pollution, the PAC needs merely to raise the tax to enhance abatement.

(9) Transferable Permits/Emission Trading

The idea for marketable pollution permits was first advanced by J.H. Dales in 1968.[16] The novel approach, while interesting to the academic community, was not incorporated into public policy until the late 1970s when the EPA set in place its offset policy with the 1977 amendments to the Clean Air Act. With the offset policy, marketable permits became one of the policy options used to abate air pollution.[17]

In principle, the PCA would allow only a certain level of polluting effluents or emissions by issuing permits -- so-called pollution certificates -- for the specified maximum amount of pollution to be allowed. The analytics of this scheme are quite straight forward. Assume that the PCA issues certificates for each type or category of pollution for a particular ecosystem. Specifically, let us assume that the PCA had established a predetermined standard that was necessary to maintain the integrity of the impacted ecosystem. Based on the relationship between that standard and an estimate of the aggregate waste emissions or effluents from all contributing sources in the region, the number of certificates to be issued is thereby determined.[18] For the sake of simplicity, let us also assume the baseline number of certificates can be annually redetermined.

With respect to our example, assume that there are several upstream firms. Each individual upstream firm (a potential purchaser of certificates) within a category of pollution will have a downward sloping demand curve for the permits, dp_i; that is, more permits will be demanded at a lower price than at a higher price (see Figure V.12). In fact, an upstream firm's demand curve for pollution certificates is its marginal pollution control costs. As can be seen from the figure, the more certificates a firm acquires, the lower will be its outlays on pollution abatement ($MPCC_i$); conversely, the fewer the certificates a firm acquires, the higher will be its outlays on pollution abatement.

The market demand curve for the pollution certificates is the horizontal summation of all of the contributing polluters in the region. The market for pollution permits will spontaneously aggregate all of the relevant pollution sources in the ecosystem and yield an effective pollution-specific market demand curve Dp (see Figure V.12). Once the PCA has determined the specified maximum amount of pollution to be allowed based on the environmental standard to be maintained, it will issue the appropriate number of marketable pollution certificates yielding an inelastic supply of permits, Sp.

As should be evident, the discipline of the market will effectively force those firms with high pollution-abatement costs to purchase more of the permits. That is, where the market price of the certificates is less than the pollution control costs, it will pay the polluting firm to buy certificates and discharge its pollution. Conversely, the low-abatement cost firms will need to purchase fewer of the

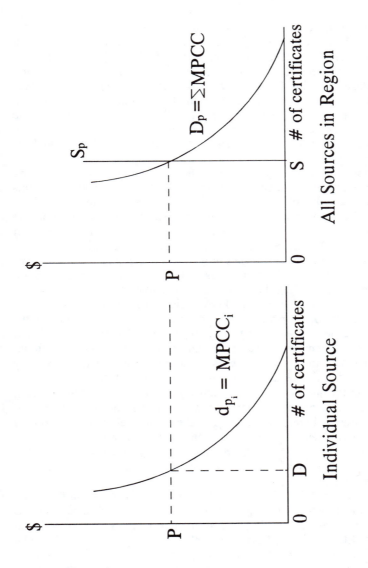

FIGURE V.12

permits inasmuch as it is cheaper for them to abate their pollution. Whenever the market price of the certificates is higher than the pollution control costs, it will pay the polluting firm to instal abatement equipment and buy fewer certificates. The combined effect is to generate a least-cost abatement solution for the region by (a) having those polluting firms who are low-cost abaters to purchase fewer permits at the initial offering, and/or (b) have the low-cost abating firms sell the certificates they may hold to the high pollution abatement cost firms (in the ongoing market). The efficiency properties of the scheme obtain due to the markets spontaneously placing the lion's share of the pollution abatement on those firms that can do so at least-cost.

In addition, potential new entrants into the ecosystem that will be emitting the specified category of pollution will effectively shift the demand for permits to the right with the effect of raising their price. Once again, the forces of the market will require the new entrants (if they are high pollution-abatement cost firms) to purchase the permits from the low-cost abaters thereby once again ensuring a least-cost solution. For the existing firms as well as new entrants, the observable market price of the certificates provides an ongoing incentive for firms to find innovative methods and technologies to reduce their marginal pollution control costs (vertically shifting their respective dp_i curves downward).

It must also be noted that if the PCA decided that the initial number of certificates offered onto the market was too great (too few) resulting in the degradation (unintended enhancement) of the regulated environmental media, it could simply annually reduce (increase) the number of certificates. In addition, the PCA could systematically alter the environmental standard by selectively entering the market and buy certificates (shifting the Sp curve marginally leftward thereby increasing the quality of the environment) or selling certificates (shifting the Sp curve marginally rightward, thereby relaxing the environmental standard). Finally, in truly free pollution permit markets, there may well be an opportunity for organized environmental groups or associations to enter the market. An environmental group could express its willingness to pay to enhance the quality of the regulated environmental media by buying up some of the certificates and holding them out of use.

As a matter of public policy in the U.S., under amendments to the Clean Air Act, pollution sources choosing to reduce emissions at discharge points beyond that necessitated by the in-place standard can apply for an emission reduction credit (ERC) from the EPA. As implied by its name, the ERC can be used to satisfy emission standards at other (more expensive) sources or sold to other existing sources as well as new incoming entrants.[19] While the ERC is essentially the "currency" used in emissions trading, four associated policies have been established that govern how these credits can be stored, transferred and spent.[20]   These policies include the offset policy, bubble policy, emissions banking, and the netting policy.

    ● Before the offset policy was set in place, the dilemma being confronted was what to do about promoting economic growth in and around metropolitan areas that were not meeting the ambient air quality standards. The offset policy requires new and expanding sources in what are deemed 'non-attainment' areas (those areas not yet meeting the specified ambient air quality standards) to secure offsetting emission reductions from existing firms or municipalities so that once the new or expanding firm goes on line, the air will be cleaner than before they began operations. That is, new or modified firms must provide for an emission reduction (offset) from an existing source(s) in the region greater than the increase in emissions due to their moving into the area of expanding their operation.

    ● The bubble policy deals primarily with existing sources and treats multiple existing emitters conceptually as if they were enclosed under a bubble. The total emissions of each air pollutant leaving the bubble are the target of regulation with the aim of achieving an overall emission reduction within the bubble. Consequently, in trying to achieve this aim, each individual source is free to abate the pollution from its own multiple point sources as it chooses; alternatively, with multiplant bubbles the trading of ERCs is allowed. In both cases it should be evident that the firm will choose a mix of abatement and acquiring ERCs (presumably a least-cost mix) as compared to having each point source conform to a uniform standard independent of cost of compliance.

    ● Netting, more a form of regulatory relief than reform, allows modifying or expanding firms to use acquired ERCs to remain within regulatory thresholds which would otherwise trigger more stringent requirements.

    ● Finally, emissions banking allows firms to store certified ECRs acquired over time and thereby enables them to be used in subsequent offset, bubble or netting programs they might chose to undertake in the future.

It has been reported that somewhere between 7,000 and 12,000 trading transactions have been consummated and that the aggregate cost savings comes to about $10 billion dollars. (Tietenberg, 1993:269).

(10) Summary

As one looks back to the various remedies that incorporate the efficiency criterion -- whether the constitutional rules, institutional working rules, communal property, the array of private property solutions as related to Coase-type bargaining or the conglomerate firm, or status rights inherent in the standards approach, effluent taxes, subsidies or tradable permits, perhaps all of this is best summed up in reviewing the summary statement made by Coase in his seminal article written some three decades ago. He stated:

> It would clearly be desirable if the only actions performed were those in which what was gained was worth more than what was lost. But in choosing between social arrangements within the context of which individual decisions are made, we have to bear in mind that a change in the existing system which will lead to an improvement in some decisions may well lead to a worsening of others. Furthermore we have to take into account the costs involved in operating the various social arrangements (whether it be the working of a market or of a government department), as well as the costs involved in moving to a new system. In devising and choosing between social arrangements we should have regard for the total effect. This, above all, is the change in approach which I am advocating (Coase, 1960:44).

ENDNOTES

1. This section and the next two are drawn from the Coase's original work (Coase, 1960) and restatements of his work including Mercuro and Ryan, (1984:76-99) and Conybeare, (1980:309-312).

2. The strong version of the Coase Theorem suggests that the allocation of resources devoted to pollution abatement *and* the allocation of resources to both good X and good Y are independent of the initial assignment of rights. The weaker version argues that while the allocation of resources devoted to pollution abatement will be the same under either rights structure, the allocation of resources to X and Y will be different but nonetheless efficient (Donohue, 1988:908-909).

3. This idea was originally presented in Coase, (1937).

4. This is one of many definitions of nuisance provided by Black, (1979: 961-962).

5. For a more complete discussion of this approach see Seneca and Taussig, (1984: 60-63).

6. This is one of many definitions of trespass provided by Black, (1979: 1346-1347).

7. Calabressi first explored this concept in Calabressi (1961) and expanded the discussion in Calabressi (1970).

8. This review draws from the works of Johnson, (1991); Mueller, (1989); McLean, (1987); and Buchanan, (1972 and 1986).

9. As documented by Buchanan, this movement toward closure has its roots in the work of Knut Wicksell and a group of Italian public finance scholars of the late 19th century including Antoio De Viti De Marco, Amilcare Puviani, Mauro Fasiana, and Matheo Pantaleoni (Buchanan, 1986:23-24 at note 117).

10. It is in this sense that Buchanan states that "There are no lines to be drawn at the edges of 'the economy' and the 'polity', or between 'markets' and 'governments', between 'the private sector' and the 'public sector'" (Buchanan, 1986:20-21).

11. As described by Buchanan, the requirement for compensation is essential, "...not in order to maintain any initial distribution on ethical grounds, but in order to decide which one from among the many possible social policy changes does, in fact, satisfy the genuine Pareto rule. Compensation is the only device available to the political economist for this purpose." (Buchanan, 1959:129).

12. For a brief historical account of environmental regulation under the U.S. E.P.A. see Portney, (1992:7-25). For a description of the essential elements of the standards approach and effluent charge approach see Freeman, (1978: 21-24).

13. For a detailed discussion of effluent charges and subsidies see Field, (1994:226-247).

14. A clear rationale for using effluent taxes is provided by Oates, (1988:5-7).

15. On the potential benefits of combining both instruments see Spence and Weitzman, (1993:205-224).

16. The first book to outline this approach was *Pollution, Property and Prices* by Dales, (1968).

17. For a detailed discussion of this approach see Field, (1994: 248-261); and for a review of assessments as to its impact regarding air pollution see Tietenberg, (1994:240-245).

18. The literature identifies three types of permit systems: (1) the ambient permit system, (2) the emissions permit system, and (3) the pollution offset system of permits (Pearce and Turner, 1990:116-117). The analytical treatment here is that of the emissions permit system. The graphical analysis presented here is similar to that presented in Downing, (1984:205-210).

19. For a brief description the institutionalized market see Hamilton, (1984: 20-21) and Weisskopf, (1989:9). A somewhat dated description of the system is provided in Lirhoff, (1980).

20. This section borrows from both Tietenberg, (1993:268-269) and Meidinger, (1985:447-479).

REFERENCES

Ackerman, B.A. and Stewart, R.B. 1988. Reforming Environmental Law: The Democratic Case for Market Incentives. In *Columbia Journal of Environmental Law*, 13 (No. 2): 171-199.

Black, H.C. 1979. *Black's Law Dictionary*. St. Paul: West Publishing Co. (4th ed.)

Buchanan, J.M. 1986. *Liberty, Market and the State*. Hertfordshire, U.K.: Harvester Press.

Buchanan, J.M. 1975. A Contractarian Paradigm for Applying Economic Theory. *American Economic Review*, 65 (May): 225-230.

Buchanan, J.M. 1972. Toward Analysis of Closed Behavioral Systems. In *Theory of Public Choice* eds. J. M. Buchanan and R. D. Tollison. Ann Arbor: University of Michigan Press: 11-23.

Buchanan, J.M. and Tullock, G. 1962. *The Calculus of Consent*. Ann Arbor: University of Michigan Press.

Buchanan, J.M. 1959. Positive Economics, Welfare Economics, and Political Economy. *Journal of Law and Economics*, 2 (October): 124-138.

Calabressi, G. 1961. Some Thoughts on Risk Distribution and the Law of Torts. *Yale Law Journal*, 70 (March): 499-553.

Calabressi, G. 1970. *The Costs of Accidents*. New Haven: Yale University Press.

Coase, R.H. 1988. *The Firm, the Market, and the Law*. Chicago: University of Chicago Press.

Coase, R.H. 1960. The Problem of Social Costs. *Journal of Law and Economics*, 3 (October): 1-44.

Coase, R.H. 1937. The Nature of the Firm. *Economica,* 4 (November): 386-408.

Conybeare, J.A.C. 1980. International Organization and the Theory of Property Rights. *International Organization*, 34 (Summer): 307-334.

Dales, J.H. 1968. *Pollution, Property and Prices*. Toronto: University of Toronto Press.

Donohue III, J.J. 1988. Law and Economics: The Road Not Taken. *Law and Society Review*, 22 (No. 5): 903-926.

Downing, P.B. 1984. *Environmental Economics and Policy*. Boston: Little Brown and Co.

Epstein, R.A. 1973. A Theory of Strict Liability. *Journal of Legal Studies*, 2 (January): 151-204.

Field, B.C. 1994. Incentive Based Strategies Emission Taxes and Subsidies; and Incentive Based Strategies Transferable Discharge Permits. Both in *Environmental Economics*, B.C. Field. New York: McGraw-Hill, Inc.

Freeman III, M.A. 1978. Air and Water Pollution Policy. In *Current Issues in U.S. Environmental Policy*, ed. P.R. Portney. Baltimore: Johns Hopkins University Press: 12-67.

Hamilton, M.M. 1984. The Air-Pollution Peddlers. *Washington Post National Weekly*, (October, 1st): 20-21.

Hardin, G. 1968. The Tragedy of the Commons. *Science*, 162 (December 13th): 1243-1248.

Johnson, D.B. 1991. *Public Choice An Introduction To The New Political Economy*. Mountain View, CA: Mayfield Publishing Co.

Landes, W.M. and Posner, R.A. 1987. *The Economic Structure of Tort Law*. Cambridge: Harvard University Press.

Liroff, R.A. 1980. *Air Pollution Offsets Trading, Selling and Banking*. Washington D.C.: Conservation Foundation.

McLean, I. 1987. *Public Choice: An Introduction*. Oxford: Basil Blackwell Ltd.

Meidinger, E. 1985. On Explaining the Development of 'Emissions Trading' in the U.S. Air Pollution Regulation, *Law & Policy*, 7 (October): 447-479.

Mercuro, N. and Ryan, T. 1984. *Law Economics and Public Policy*. Greenwich, CT: JAI Press.

Mueller, D.C. 1989. *Public Choice-II*. Cambridge: Cambridge University Press.

Oates, W.E. 1988. Taxing Pollution An Idea Whose Time Has Come, *Resources*, Washington, D.C.: Resources for the Future: 5-7.

Ostrom, E. 1990. *Governing the Commons*. Cambridge: Cambridge University Press.

Pearce, D.W, and Turner, R.K. 1990. *Economics of Natural Resources and the Environment*. Baltimore: Johns Hopkins University Press.

Pigou, A.C. 1952 [reprint]. *The Economics of Welfare*. London: Macmilliam and Co.

Portney, P.R. 1992. EPA and the Evolution of Federal Regulation. In *Public Policies for Environmental Protection*, ed. P.R. Portney. Washington, D.C. Johns Hopkins University Press: 7-25.

Posner, R.A. 1986. *The Economic Analysis of Law*. Boston: Little, Brown and Co.

Posner, R.A. 1973. Strict Liability: A Comment. *Journal of Legal Studies*, 2 (January): 205-221.

Reisman, D. 1990. *The Political Economy of James Buchanan*. College Station: Texas A & M University Press.

Schoenbaum, T.J. 1985. *Environmental Policy Law*. Mineola: Foundation Press, Inc.

Seneca, J.J. and Taussig, M.K. 1984. *Environmental Economics*. Englewood Cliffs, N.J.: Prentice-Hall Inc.

Spence, A.M. and Weitzman, M.L. 1993. Regulatory Strategies for Pollution Control. In *Economics of the Environment Selected Readings*, eds. R. Dorfman and N.S. Dorfman. New York: Norton Press: 205-224.

Stewart, R.B. 1988. Controlling Environmental Risks Through Economic Incentives. *Columbia Journal of Environmental Law*, 13 (No. 2): 153-169.

Tietenberg, T.H. 1994. *Environmental Economics and Policy*. New York: Harper Collins College Publishers.

Tietenberg, T.H. 1993. Economic Instruments for Environmental Regulation. In *Environmental Economics A Reader*, eds. A. Markandya and J. Richardson. New York: St. Martin's Press: 267-286.

Weisskopf, M. 1989. The Pollution Peddlers. *Washington Post National Weekly*, (November, 20th): 20.

INDEX

ABOUT THE AUTHORS

Nicholas Mercuro holds a B.A. degree in economics from Pennsylvania State University, a M.B.A. degree from Seton Hall University, and in 1977, was awarded a Ph.D. from the Department of Resource Development at Michigan State University. Since 1976, he has been on the faculty of the Department of Economics and Finance at the University of New Orleans where he is presently full professor of economics.

He has authored several journal articles, book chapters and book reviews in the field of law and economics. He has also co-authored a theoretical exploration into the field titled *Law, Economics and Public Policy* published by JAI Press in 1984. In 1989, with Kluwer Academic Publishers, he edited a collection of essays for a book titled *Law and Economics*. The collection of original essays describes the development, tensions, and prospects for the several schools of thought that presently comprise the field of Law and Economics. In addition, also with Kluwer Academic Publishers, Professor Mercuro has edited a collection of original articles titled *Taking Property and Just Compensation: Law and Economics Perspectives of the Takings Issue*. The collection analyzes U.S. Supreme Court decisions regarding the takings clause of the 5th Amendment to the U.S. Constitution.

In 1986-1987 Professor Mercuro was a visiting professor at the Institute of Economic Theory at the University of Vienna. Since 1988 he has been a member of the adjunct faculty at the Tulane Law School where he teaches The Economics of Legal Relationships. In 1989 he founded, and now serves as the series editor of an inter-disciplinary annual journal, entitled *International Review of Comparative Public Policy*. In the Spring of 1993 Professor Mercuro taught at the Free University of Berlin as a Fulbright Scholar.

Franklin A. López holds a B.S. and M.S. in Chemical Engineering from the University of Texas at Austin, an M.A. in Economics from the University of Texas at Arlington, and a Ph.D. in Economics from Tulane University. Since 1976 he has been a member of the economics faculty at the University of New Orleans where he is now an Associate Professor. He has also taught at the Escuela Politécnica Nacional in Quito and the Instituto de Desarrollo Empresarial in Guayaquil, Ecuador. He has extensive experience in the economic evaluation of public and private projects.

He has authored several journal articles and book chapters in economic development and international monetary economics. He is co-author of *Economía al alcance de todos* published in 1992 by Harper-Row Latinoamericana. Sice

1990 he has served as the Associate Editor of *Que Pasa New Orleans*, a monthly Spanish magazine. He is also a syndicated columnist, his op-ed articles appear in 40 newspapers in 11 Latin American countries, through the *Agencia Interamericana de Prensa Económica*; since 1988 he has served as a weekly columnist for "El Universo", the largest daily newspaper of Ecuador. Several of his monographs have been published by the Centro de Estudios Económico-Sociales of Guatemala and the Instituto Ecuatoriano de Economía Política.

Kristian P. Preston received a B.A. from the University of California at Berkeley, a M.A. from the University of California at Los Angeles, and was awarded a Ph.D. from the Department of Geography at the University of California at Los Angeles in 1986. He is currently an Associate Professor of geography at the University of New Orleans.

He has published several journal articles and book chapters on the effects of air pollution on Mediterranean-type ecosystems and community level responses to air pollution. His current research in this area focuses on the effects of air pollution on ecosystem resilience. Over the past three years he has also conducted collaborative research on the effects of shoreline alteration, urban runoff, and marsh deterioration on the structure and function of submerged aquatic vegetation in Lake Pontchartrain, Louisiana.